INSPIRING COMMITMENT

How to Win Employee Loyalty in Chaotic Times

Anthony Mendes

IRWIN

Professional Publishing

*Chicago • Bogotá •Boston • Buenos Aires • Caracas
London • Madrid •Mexico City • Sydney • Toronto*

This publication is designed to provide accurate and authoritative information in regard to the subject matter covered. It is sold with the understanding that neither the author or the publisher is engaged in rendering legal, accounting, or other professional service. If legal advice or other expert assistance is required, the services of a competent professional person should be sought.

From a Declaration of Principles jointly adopted by a Committee of the American Bar Association and a Committee of Publishers.

Irwin Professional Book Team

Publisher: *Wayne McGuirt*
Senior sponsoring editor: *Cynthia A. Zigmund*
Developmental editor: *Pat Muller*
Marketing manager: *Kelly Sheridan*
Managing editor: *Kevin Thornton*
Project editor: *Denise Santor-Mitzit*
Production supervisor: *Pat Frederickson*
Prepress buyer: *Jon Christopher*
Jacket designer: *Shot in the Dark Design*
Compositor: *ElectraGraphics, Inc.*
Typeface: *11/14 Palatino*
Printer: *Quebecor/Fairfield*

◤▰ **Times Mirror**
Ⓜ **Higher Education Group**

ISBN: 0-7863-0422-7

Printed in the United States of America
1 2 3 4 5 6 7 8 9 0 QF 2 1 0 9 8 7 6 5

DEDICATION

Dedicated to my parents, Arthur and Adela, for your unwavering commitment to each other and to the well being of your children. Your love and belief in my abilities enabled me to pursue my dreams.

Also to my wife and partner, Jody. Thank you for a shared vision and the work you put into this book. It wouldn't have happened without you.

ABOUT ANTHONY MENDES

Anthony Mendes has been a student in two games. A 13 year career with AT&T working in the areas of organizational change, personal resource development, and organizational stress initiatives has created an in-depth base of knowledge of the way people operate within organizations. Serving as a consultant to other major corporations such as Ford Motor Company and the Commonwealth Imperial Bank of Canada has provided a diverse perspective on the dynamics of change in the world of business. While at AT&T, Dr. Mendes coordinated the landmark pilot health study, Total Life Concept (TLC), the most comprehensively evaluated corporate health promotion study in the U.S.

Mendes has also explored commitment on a more intimate and personal level in the context of private psychotherapy practice. His frame of reference emphasizes that both psychological and physical health are defined and maintained by the capacity for self-renewal.

Having learned about the value of hard work and persistence from his immigrant parents, Mendes earned his own way to both undergraduate and masters degrees in psychology from Central Missouri State University. He then worked as a counselor for the division of occupational rehabilitation of the Missouri state department of education for several years before making a commitment to earn his Ph.D.—which involved selling his house to finance the project. He earned his doctorate in 1985 from the University of Missouri.

Dr. Mendes is currently adjunct professor at Rutgers University's medical school, the University of Medicine and Dentistry of New Jersey, and at Polytechnic University in Brooklyn, New York. He is a frequent lecturer and seminar presenter at national training conferences. Mendes maintains a strong personal commitment to his marriage and family (he is the father of two small children) and to maintaining a high level of personal health and fitness. He has run several marathons and considers regular exercise and a healthy diet to be crucial to his success in all areas of life.

PREFACE

As both a psychologist and a 13 year veteran of the corporate world, I have been witness to enormous economic and cultural change in the past decade. Most importantly, I have seen the very personal impact of these changes on *people*. It has become clear to me that individuals can only perform their work excellently when they are fully committed to it. This is impossible unless the work environment effectively embraces change as it affects *lives*, not simply business. Managers are learning that it is no longer practical or profitable for people to completely separate work from health and/or family. In fact, the most successful workers can be found in an environment that supports a balance of all three. This book was written for today's business professionals, to be understood in the context of both their work and personal lives.

Inspiring Commitment is designed to help you view and experience your commitments in a new way. It can be used to assess commitment, personal as well as work related, and the exercises it contains will help to create a strategy based on areas of strength and weakness. In this sense, *Inspiring Commitment* is a tool for both individuals and groups. It is written in a nontechnical and nonclinical manner for easy application by a wide span of employees, from CEO to the first line manager. By focusing on the four key factors of commitment, a group, organization, or an individual can better the chances of maintaining true commitment and not temporary lip service.

Anthony Mendes, Ph.D.

CONTENTS

1

THE ENERGY CRISIS IN AMERICAN BUSINESS

Imagine your boss entering your office on a Friday and announcing, "I just want to remind you we can fire you at any time if you don't produce. And even if you do produce, there might be layoffs because of industry cutbacks. But work hard—we've got lots of customers to please. I'm depending on you. And by the way, I don't expect any of your family responsibilities to interfere with your work. Around here we leave our personal lives at the door. And one more thing: here's a project I need you to complete over the weekend."

Sound a little bit like, You're important to our goals, and we expect you to give us your best, but don't expect any security or respect in return for your efforts? Even though no responsible manager would ever actually use these words, these are the messages being communicated by corporate America to its workers. No wonder they're confused . . . and disloyal.

An insidious crisis is infecting the American workplace, draining job performance, quality, and profitability. The same crisis has spread to personal lifestyles and to relationships. It isn't just about an uncertain stock market, massive layoffs, or global competitiveness. The crisis arises from within the individual. It is a lack of commitment.

The word *commitment* sounds interesting when it's bandied about at a motivational meeting, or takes on depth when spoken in grave tones by a powerful CEO, but most workers don't understand the concept. Commitment is far more than just being loyal. It springs from deep within the psyche. As Eleanor Roosevelt once said, "One's philosophy is not best expressed in words. It is expressed in the choices one makes . . . And the choices we make are ultimately our responsibility." Commitment can be influenced by external forces—such as a corporate culture or even a manager with an enlightened perspective.

A midwestern pharmaceutical company that I worked with several years ago typifies this idea. The manager came to me because of low morale and slacking sales. It seemed that a recent merger and subsequent reorganizations might be responsible for this, but he wasn't sure what to do about it. Based on information from focus groups and interviews with the sales force, I determined that the impact of the merger had made itself felt in the following ways:

- No one was sure where the company was headed or how they fit into the picture.

- Lack of communication led to suspicion, anxiety, and distrust.

- The division manager continued to support products that were in direct competition with the merging company's products.

- Emotions ran high as people resented decisions being made with an apparent lack of concern for people who were affected by them.

- In saying one thing and doing another, management was weak in follow-through.

- Most people were waiting for the company to "get its act together" and had little motivation to perform.

GUARANTEES GONE

Commitment hasn't faltered simply because the American worker has become more lazy. In fact, the opposite is true. Today's worker puts in longer hours and assumes more responsibility in a fast-paced, stressful work environment.

Commitment was more automatic decades ago when companies handed over job security in exchange for hard work. In today's competitive environment, that guarantee is no longer offered—even for high-level executives—and as a result, the traditional corporate loyalty has been replaced by skepticism and uncertainty.

Valuable energy that was once channeled creatively and productively is being diverted to cope with the stress of financial and professional insecurity. Efforts to help employees cope often take the form of task-oriented direction or inconsistent and insincere statements of reassurance. What is missing is a full understanding of the emotional impact on the American worker as these changes occur. The only effective strategies for gaining loyalty are those that incorporate this understanding, and it is imperative that it be communicated in a genuine and sincere manner.

There is a personal price that individuals pay as commitments falter. Self-esteem is diminished as people begin to question the purpose and meaning of their work. Families and close relationships feel the strain as tempers are shortened and time together is overshadowed by anxiety and tension. Physical symptoms of stress take their toll and show up as insomnia, headaches, stomach problems, and numerous other ailments as well as increased on-the-job accidents. Skyrocketing disability claims are draining both financial and human resources in the public and private sectors of American business (New Jersey's *Star Ledger* newspaper, July 30th, 1995). Absence due to illness only adds to the employee's sense of being out of control and vulnerable.

▌ SHIFTING SANDS

The number of companies laying off people in recent years is so extensive they could hardly be listed here. Politicians and executives talk about job retraining and moving laid-off people to new areas, but on the street that means former white-collar managers are learning to say, You want fries with that?

One laid-off worker reports sending a mass mailing of 2,000 resumes to get a job. High-performance employees tell of receiving a 2 percent raise (the company's highest) because of company money problems. Workers complain tiredly at coffee break of their previous evening—running errands, doing laundry, helping kids with homework, then sandwiching in an hour or two of extra work brought home.

In my private practice a midlevel manager was referred to me for symptoms of depression. He reported feelings of failure, inadequacy, and helplessness along with the more traditional physical symptoms of insomnia, loss of appetite, and lethargy. At work he performed at a minimum, kept a low profile, and basically decided to coast until reassignment or, if he could make it, retirement. He had given up any hope of advancement or promotion and felt disconnected from the goals and objectives of his work group. He stated that he wanted to spend more time with his family but also felt guilty and tense around them because of his disappointing job. A significant part of the therapeutic process involved helping him to redefine himself as a person. The career that had been his primary source of self-esteem and identity was no longer meeting those needs. A more realistic set of expectations and a shift in focus from promotion and advancement to job satisfaction helped to revitalize his motivation and energy.

Researchers cite the following facts about today's workforce:

- A 1993 study by the Families and Work Institute reported that:

  42 percent of employees experienced downsizing in their companies;

  20 percent feared they'd lose their jobs;

  42 percent felt exhausted by the end of the work day.

- Northwestern National Life Insurance Company conducted studies of 1,900 employees in 1991–92 and found that 40 percent of private-sector workers (that's nearly half!) felt their jobs were "very" or "extremely" stressful.

- One-third of employees actually expected to burn out in the near future.

▌ WHAT HAPPENED AT WORK?

Decades ago, the workforce (heavily male, mostly white) was slower paced. Global competition was almost unheard of. The traditional one-income family was the norm and working hours were shorter, so balancing work and home was not an issue. Over the years, though, companies have had to work harder and smarter to survive. Our economy has changed and continues to change, more quickly and more dramatically than ever before.

These factors and many others have reshaped the workplace. What we have today is a business environment that demands more from people. Misguided companies have tried to crack the whip with the threat of unemployment, to no avail. Job-hopping has become commonplace, with the average manager working for 8 to 10 different companies during the course of a career. Fear of job loss, while keeping some employees in place, only keeps them in an unhappy place where they will survive with minimum productivity.

As the old ways of doing business fade away, old-fashioned company loyalty is disappearing as well. Many work styles have changed, creating a workplace that looks dramatically different from the way it was decades ago.

There is another major force that is reshaping commitment. Our society is changing dramatically as well, and along with it, our personal roles and responsibilities change. Because women have moved strongly into the workforce, the work/home balance has become a major issue for both men and women. Simultaneously, male baby boomers, the first spawn of the modern nuclear family, realize their upbringing of mom-at-home, dad-never-around was not ideal for building their own masculine identity. These men want more time at home. They want to be participative parents. They refuse to consistently work extra hours in the evening or on weekends, and they begin to resent their employer when pressured to do so.

VICTIMIZATION

Despite the temporary problems that have resulted, these changes are often good ones. Under the old contract, complacency and inefficiency were often the byproducts of security. People expected and received promotions, pay increases, and other assorted perks based on years spent on the job. The result was an unhealthy dependency, which did not always foster initiative and self-responsibility. Rewards and incentives based on outstanding achievement were sometimes secondary to standard rewards based on tenure. A current manifestation of this dependency is the growing number of people expressing outrage at being "victimized" by corporate change.

In working with employees in a national telecommunications company, I was struck by the number of people experiencing and expressing this victimization. Many of them had come to take for granted generous health care benefits, stock options, retirement plans, and regular pay raises and bonuses. Typically, a standard 5 percent annual raise could be expected for basic satisfactory job performance. (Incidentally, a job rating of "far exceeding expectation" would only warrant an additional $200 to $300 bonus. For someone earning about $50,000, this was only .5 percent.)

Obviously this system was a disincentive for employees to put in an additional 10 to 15 hours work per week required for outstanding performance. In conducting "Managing Change" seminars, I noticed an interesting relationship between an employee's job performance and that employee's level of outrage in dealing with potential job loss. It seemed that employees who were content with average performance operated out of a belief that the company "owed" them not only job security but the standard raises and benefits as well. The more outstanding performers were markedly less angry and seemed able to see beyond the current crisis. They were more inclined to explore alternative options in the absence of guaranteed employment.

It was clear to me that there was an intrinsic benefit for these individuals in sustaining high performance. Their personal sense of responsibility and self-worth empowered them to face possible termination of employment without wasting energy on blame and resentment. Despite the normal emotional reaction to pending job loss (anyone in this situation feels profoundly concerned and anxious), they were not burdened by the additional emotional baggage of hostility, helplessness, and hopelessness.

The key difference between the dependent victimized employee and the self-confident and empowered one lies in a personal sense of commitment.

FAMILY ISSUES

A new introduction of family issues into the corporate culture is also breathing life into work values. As workers are finding support for family-related needs, they are responding with greater appreciation for their companies and renewed loyalty. Recent surveys are showing improvements in satisfaction and morale as a result of family-friendly policies and initiatives (*Recommiting the Workforce*. Work Family Directions, 1994).

More recognition and participation is sought by today's employees. Since there is no guarantee of long-term employment—a former identity badge for an individual—workers ask for projects that can create a sense of achievement. Having adjusted to a more fast-paced society, employees simply aren't as willing to endure boring work.

Improved technology has placed us as hitchhikers of sorts all along the information highway. Rapidly obtained, accessible information is another demand placed on today's worker. Witness the enormous growth of the training business. Few people needed job training in 1950 once they were already on the job—after all, you simply had to do your job and you had a secure spot anyway. But today, even employees who plan to stay with their employers want learning opportunities. Growth and career improvement are seen as necessary, much like a loaded gun was for our ancestors, in case of a wild animal attack. The wild animals in today's market are sudden job loss and stagnating careers.

MORE DEMANDS ON FEWER PEOPLE

Though the expectation of a company being loyal to an employee by guaranteeing job security and regular advancement has long since evaporated, the demands on the employee for performance have increased dramatically. This new era of more intense corporate competition has necessitated better customer service and higher productivity with less error. In some ways, it seems as if the focus has shifted radically from how executives wanted to do things to how the customer wants the company to do things—entirely skipping over the needs of most workers.

With companies unable to guarantee job security or promotions, and demanding more and better work from fewer people, a crunch has occurred. "Flatter" organizations have failed to effectively maintain employee loyalty and endure high turnover and poor productivity, considering them necessary evils. Conversely, inspiring loyalty—at least the new loyalty—is proven a superior path. Some facts:

• A study conducted in 1993 by AT&T showed that 70 percent of customer satisfaction depended on the service the customer received from the employee rather than the satisfaction with the product itself.

• Sixty-five percent of problems in customer service occur because of indifferent or unhelpful employees, says a 1991 study of the Forum Corporation. Only 14 percent of problems were due to a product of poor quality.

Clearly, there is a link between lack of commitment and a lessening of work quality.

On a personal level, I have noticed changes in our local supermarket. For many years it was the "only game in town," and drew customers from a wide area. This allowed the owners to enjoy substantial profits despite providing poor service. It was common to overhear comments exchanged between employees who were resentful and disrespectful of management. These same employees behaved in an irritable and lethargic manner when asked by a customer for assistance and information. Several months ago a new store opened on the other side of town. This store demonstrated a high level of customer service and a pleasant atmosphere. Employees seemed to enjoy what they were doing and to be sincerely interested in the needs of the customer. Subsequently, there was a noticeable drop in the number of cars in the parking lot of the old store. Recently, I stopped in to pick up something at the old store and observed a significant difference in the behavior of both employees and management. People smiled, asked if I needed help, and thanked me for shopping there. Obviously, the store owner had belatedly become aware of the relationship between morale, quality service, and profits.

THE NEW LOYALTY

Does our current situation mean employees will never be committed to their jobs again? No. The rules have simply changed. The blind loyalty that was part of the typical business trade-off (work hard for our company and we guarantee you a job) is gone. But today's workers can have a new type of loyalty ignited within them.

Managers who take the right steps in handling their employees will win this new loyalty. It involves providing:

- Flexibility for work/home concerns.

- Opportunities for learning and career enhancement.

- Disclosure (to some extent) with regard to the direction and goals of the organization.

- Knowledge of where each employee can contribute to the overall goal.

- A chance to be part of the decision-making process.

- Interesting work.

- Positive, fact-based feedback including recognition for good work.

- Respectful, two-way communication in a more collaborative work environment.

The rewards for the manager are abundant: better performance, better job satisfaction (leading to reduced turnover), fresh creativity, less energy and money spent on personnel problems, improved image for the company (both internally and externally), and much more initiative on the part of the employee.

THE TRAINING CONUNDRUM

Many companies have used training to improve employee relations and boost morale. Specific skill-based training will continue to be an important and necessary component of human resource development.

During the 1970s another form of training emerged in an attempt to build worker loyalty. The popularity of motivational training lay in its focus on the emotional aspects of work. This stratum of training is a major industry today and runs the gamut from highly effective applied training that makes a real difference within a company to cookie-cutter seminars and fluffy motivational speeches that offer a quick-fix approach. Any training experience can be beneficial, but more and more managers are tired of spending dollars on training that seems to evaporate. It is common for seminar participants to return very quickly to old patterns of behavior after a fleeting burst of enthusiasm.

This book will help any manager acquire a deeper understanding of commitment—how to inspire it, how to enhance it, how to manage it. Sustained commitment can only be achieved through a combination of organizational, management, and individual influences. You can't just send a few workers to a seminar and hope they come back committed—especially if no significant changes have occurred within your organization. The employees may only be motivated to change for a short period of time (if at all), then unable once again to be fully productive because they're facing the same frustrations as before.

Making these changes and making them work are major challenges, and many managers haven't had the necessary tools to meet them. There has been little research on commitment until recently. Under the old system, when loyalty was more automatic, there wasn't a need to analyze it. Today's workplace demands that analysis. That's one reason the Commitment Factor Profile was created. This unique Profile and instructions for its use are covered in the next chapter. By using the Profile and gaining an understanding of the components of commitment, you'll be able to create this new loyalty within your organization and within yourself.

WHAT EXACTLY IS COMMITMENT?

Commitment is a set of reliable, predictable, and dedicated behaviors that separate success from failure. Having a high level of commitment is a desirable trait that can lead a person to success in both the professional and personal realms. It shouldn't be confused with other factors that can contribute to success. For example:

Decisiveness is not commitment—the ability to make a decision is easier than sustaining a commitment to it. Because we're a nation that rewards a sort of muscular aggressiveness (especially in the business world), most of us have become better able to make decisions than workers of decades ago. But *making* decisions is one thing—*sticking* to them is quite another. Witness the U.S. divorce rate: 50 percent. It's easy to get married . . . difficult to stay married till death do you part.

Ambition is not commitment—they can go hand in hand, but ambition can run amuck. True commitment means dedication and incorporates personal integrity, whereas ambition can mean railroading over other people to get to the top.

Obligation is not commitment—obligation implies that one *ought* to do something. Commitment means the self-motivation to see something through. It works both inside and outside the concept of ought—after all, many people don't do what they ought to do because they don't have the commitment.

A *Guarantee* is not commitment—commitment relies on effort to reach a particular goal or fulfill a decision, but commitment is not a guarantee. Meeting a long-term goal can be a slippery trail with setbacks and mishaps. A person with commitment runs a chance of not reaching success exactly as expected. What commitment will do is help keep a person on track toward success and aligned with personal values and needs.

▌ MOVING TO HOME

The commitment crisis that took place in the office has also crept into American homes. Personal relationships with spouses and family members have crumbled under the weight of societal changes. The old strings that held people in place—church, family traditions, community morals—have weakened and changed considerably.

The result? A slew of support groups and self-help books, an interest in trendy or other-worldly solutions, and more people seeking counseling to prop up the shattered skeletons of their lives.

Granted, we're a more open society, more tolerant of mental health counseling, and more willing to handle problems outside the family setting. But many of these so-called solutions don't work because the commitment isn't there. Lifestyle changes like weight loss are a good example. How many people do you know who start a diet, then later start another, and another? It can become a revolving door of special frozen foods, attending classes, and buying accoutrements like food weight scales. What all of these attempts at change have in common is that people tend to look to the program, the book, or some other *external* source to improve the quality of their lives. With commitment, however, the process is personal and powerful . . . and a lot more permanent. Significant *internal* changes occur with true commitment, and sustained *personal* responsibility is an integral part of real success.

Developing a stronger level of commitment at work can teach you, or teach another, how to bring the same strong commitment home, and the reverse is true as well.

Success generates success. When people come to understand commitment and employ it, they develop the power
to truly take control of their lives, to live out their core values and realize their fullest potential as human beings.
Opening the door to this type of optimal living is the commitment I have made in writing this book.

2

THE COMMITMENT FACTOR

My early interest in the area of commitment began with the frustration and wonder that grew out of my work in the field of health promotion. As a researcher and implementer of wellness programs for a large telecommunications company, I was proud of the initial success we had in helping employees change their lifestyle habits. The first year of programming resulted in very significant changes: people losing weight, exercising, effectively managing their stress, and reducing cholesterol levels through reduced-fat dieting. My frustration grew out of the fact that much of the success was short-lived and people gradually resorted back to their old ways and lifestyles. This continues to be the major challenge facing health professionals today. How do we get people to stick with their new healthy lifestyles?

This challenge led to my initial exploration of the research in this area. I conducted my first computerized literature search in 1986, and much to my surprise, found nothing in the psychological literature. Subsequent searches in the following years produced little on the subject of commitment. I soon realized that a major reason for this lack of information was the fact that there was no instrument or tool that specifically measured commitment and no concrete definition of what it meant. In 1987, while working with Dr. Mark Tager, a well-known author and expert in the field of health promotion, we began to ask the question, What is commitment?

This began as a simple process of literally asking hundreds of people for their interpretation or definition of commitment. With this information I developed a list of items that seemed to capture what people were saying. Through further analysis we determined that there were four factors or categories that these items fell into, namely, vision, insight, acceptance, and integration. The commitment questionnaire is the final result of several years of reworking items and determining the 20 items that are most highly related to perceptions of commitment. More than 2,500 individuals have completed this questionnaire to create the present form. It is designed specifically to be easy to complete, easy to understand, and helpful in determining areas in which improving commitment is needed. The commitment questionnaire can be used in a business setting, for assessing relationship commitments, or for determining the strength of commitment in any major area of a person's life. As a personal note, the instrument was especially helpful to my wife in determining commitment to motherhood and having our first child. We determined areas of strength and also areas for concern (especially when it came to a shared vision for parenting).

In the business setting I have found the questionnaire especially helpful in team development and group performance. Tallying the scores to create a Group Profile is especially helpful to the manager interested in gaining consensus and commitment. In my private practice I have used it extensively with couples, in career counseling, and in modifying health behaviors.

▋ USES OF THE PROFILE

The Commitment Profile can be used in a variety of contexts and is applicable to numerous personal and professional issues. Printed copies of the Profile for ongoing use are available by contacting Anthony Mendes, Ph.D., at (908) 689-3087.

Here are some specific examples of ways in which the Profile may be used:

- Manager takes it himself to measure his own commitment in a particular area.

- Manager gives it to employee to measure commitment on a particular task or project, or to assess overall commitment to the job. Results are discussed together.

- Manager gives it to employee for the purposes listed on the item above, but employee reviews his own results privately.

- Personal applications are used by manager or employees, results shared or not. For instance, if a company has a work wellness program in place and a participant is not confident about his ability to stick to an exercise program, the Profile could be used to gauge the participant's current level of commitment.

The Profile was designed to be used in three primary areas: work, relationships, and health. The following are some examples of commitments that could be examined:

WORK:

> Shared responsibility with a committee or group
>
> Taking on a new role or project (may include relocation)
>
> Adapting to a reorganization
>
> Improving relations with supervisor or subordinate

RELATIONSHIPS:

> Becoming a better spouse
>
> Giving more time to family
>
> Improving relations with extended family
>
> Parenthood

HEALTH:

> Quitting smoking
>
> Eating for health or weight control
>
> Eliminating abuse of alcohol or drugs
>
> Beginning exercise program

These are just a few examples. Reviewing personal goals or those of an organization and its employees may reveal additional needs. Some managers prefer to keep copies of completed profiles in a folder, then re-administer the Profile on the same topic at a later date. This can indicate whether commitment has improved or changed, and can be used to evaluate training or other programs directed at enhancing commitment.

▌ PRESENTING THE IDEA

Though we're rapidly becoming a nation of assessment tool-takers, there are still many individuals who are reluctant to participate in such evaluations. Some people still see them as personality tests or fear that managers have a secret key or other mechanism to reveal deep meanings beneath what's seen on the paper.

This Profile has no such hidden agenda. What the participant sees is what he gets. The instrument is also simple to understand and self-score.

THE COMMITMENT FACTOR PROFILE

Assess your level of commitment to a particular decision. First, list at the top the commitment you would like to assess. Then read each statement and enter the corresponding number that best describes how true the statement is for you. As you complete each section, total the numbers entered to determine the score for that section.

The commitment is: _____

SECTION A

Strongly Agree	Agree	Somewhat Agree	Disagree	
4	3	2	1	
___	___	___	___	I have a clear vision of where I am heading with this commitment.
___	___	___	___	I can anticipate positive benefits of this commitment.
___	___	___	___	This commitment allows me to do something that is personally meaningful.
___	___	___	___	If I were to share my image or vision with another who is involved in this goal with me, we would have a similar picture.
___	___	___	___	I am committed for reasons important to me, not to satisfy others.
___	___	___	___	*Total each column*

Add each column total and enter it here: Total Score Section A ____

SECTION B

4	3	2	1	
___	___	___	___	What I have learned from my past experiences enables me to carry out this commitment.
___	___	___	___	There are things that I do to prevent old behaviors from getting in the way of my success.
___	___	___	___	I know how to modify my habits to make this commitment last.
___	___	___	___	I have a plan for dealing with barriers that interfere with this commitment.
___	___	___	___	There are things that I do on a daily basis to keep this commitment alive.
___	___	___	___	*Total each column*

Add each column total and enter it here: Total Score Section B ____

SECTION C

4	3	2	1	
__	__	__	__	I willingly give up pleasures of the moment to gain something better in the long term.
__	__	__	__	I am willing to face the fears, frustrations, and disappointments associated with this commitment.
__	__	__	__	The rewards of this commitment are worth the sacrifices I make to keep it going.
__	__	__	__	I recognize and value the small steps I take in achieving this commitment.
__	__	__	__	Being committed in this area makes my life more satisfying.
__	__	__	__	*Total each column*

Add each column total and enter it here: Total Score Section C _____

SECTION D

4	3	2	1	
__	__	__	__	People observing my behavior can see that I am committed.
__	__	__	__	I make positive statements to others about my success in this area.
__	__	__	__	I believe I have the ability to keep this commitment going.
__	__	__	__	When it comes to this commitment, I do what I say I am going to do.
__	__	__	__	I know what to do to be successful in this commitment and I am consistent in doing it.
__	__	__	__	*Total each column*

Add each column total and enter it here: Total Score Section D _____

COMMITMENT PROFILE

Transfer your total score from sections A, B, C, and D into the slots below:

_____	+	_____	+	_____	+	_____	=	_____
A		B		C		D		Total
Vision		Insight		Acceptance		Integration		Commitment Score

UNDERSTANDING YOUR COMMITMENT SCORES

If your score in any commitment factor is:

0-8   You are low in this particular factor. It will be difficult to maintain your commitment if you do not improve in this area.

9-13   You are fairly low in this area, but you are doing some things right. Although you might feel committed at times, you need to improve this area to avoid setbacks.

14-17   You are fairly consistent in this area and will enjoy some success. There are, however, pitfalls of which you are unaware.

18-20   You are committed in this factor. This area is one of your strengths. Rely on it when the going gets tough.

If your total commitment score is:

0-24   You need to reconsider this commitment.

25-44   You will probably find it difficult to maintain your commitment. But this book can help you make changes necessary for success.

45-64   Your commitment may falter. Work through this book, paying special attention to the factors where you scored the lowest.

65-80   You have an excellent chance of maintaining your commitment.

▌ THE COMMITMENT FACTOR PROFILE IN ACTION

Let's take a look at a particular situation in which the Profile was used. Scott, a midlevel manager, questioned the commitment of one of his staff members, Jack. Jack seemed to perform just adequately enough to get by in his job, earning only average performance reviews. He expressed a desire to be promoted and to grow professionally, yet Scott occasionally heard Jack audibly voicing opposition to management's decisions and expectations. Jack had the potential to take on more responsibility—if he could prove himself to be motivated.

When an opportunity arose to manage a new order fulfillment unit, Scott offered Jack the position on a temporary basis. For the first time Jack would supervise a couple of people, and do some of the work himself. Scott could not afford major errors on Jack's part—it was part of a new company-wide effort at improved customer service. Scott decided to use the Commitment Factor Profile to assess Jack's personal investment in the success of the effort. Jack agreed to be honest in his replies so that he could better understand his own commitment to taking on the task.

The results:

SECTION A

Strongly Agree	Agree	Somewhat Agree	Disagree	
4	3	2	1	
—	—	✓	—	I have a clear vision of where I am heading with this commitment.
—	✓	—	—	I can anticipate positive benefits of this commitment.
—	—	✓	—	This commitment allows me to do something that is personally meaningful.
—	✓	—	—	If I were to share my image or vision with another who is involved in this goal with me, we would have a similar picture.
—	—	✓	—	I am committed for reasons important to me, not to satisfy others.
—	6	6	—	*Total each column*

Add each column total and enter it here: Total Score Section A **12**

SECTION B

4	3	2	1	
—	—	✓	—	What I have learned from my past experiences enables me to carry out this commitment.
—	—	—	✓	There are things that I do to prevent old behaviors from getting in the way of my success..
—	—	✓	—	I know how to modify my habits to make this commitment last.
—	—	—	✓	I have a plan for dealing with barriers that interfere with this commitment.
—	—	✓	—	There are things that I do on a daily basis to keep this commitment alive.
—	—	6	2	*Total each column*

Add each column total and enter it here: Total Score Section B **8**

SECTION C

4	3	2	1	
—	✓	—	—	I willingly give up pleasures of the moment to gain something better in the long term.
—	✓	—	—	I am willing to face the fears, frustrations, and disappointments associated with this commitment.
—	—	✓	—	The rewards of this commitment are worth the sacrifices I make to keep it going.

		✓		I recognize and value the small steps I take in achieving this commitment.
		✓		Being committed in this area makes my life more satisfying.
	6	**6**		*Total each column*

Add each column total and enter it here: Total Score Section C   **12**

SECTION D

4	3	2	1	
		✓		People observing my behavior can see that I am committed.
			✓	I make positive statements to others about my success in this area.
		✓		I believe I have the ability to keep this commitment going.
		✓		When it comes to this commitment, I do what I say I am going to do.
		✓		I know what to do to be successful in this commitment and I am consistent in doing it.
		8	**1**	*Total each column*

Add each column total and enter it here: Total Score Section D   **9**

COMMITMENT PROFILE

Transfer your total score from sections A, B, C, and D into the slots below:

12	+	**8**	+	**12**	+	**9**	=	**41**
A		B		C		D		Total
Vision		Insight		Acceptance		Integration		Commitment Score

Jack was dismayed, and somewhat surprised, at the results of his profile. He realized his commitment to managing the new order fulfillment unit was not very strong. When Scott discussed this with him, Jack's true feelings came to the surface: he felt strong pressure from others (particularly his spouse) to achieve in his career and be more financially successful. Jack had also come from a highly competitive family. His brothers, in fact, were doing quite well in business, and Jack felt inadequate. These personal issues were directly affecting Jack's work performance. He was attempting to commit to a career-path vision that wasn't really his own, and was finding it difficult to follow through consistently.

Through further discussion, Jack eventually realized that he needed to build self-esteem to enjoy his job and feel good about it, and to define his own career goals. He had to decide how he could feel successful personally and worry less about appearing successful to others, particularly his family members. He decided to pass on this job advancement opportunity until he was ready for something he really wanted for himself. Then he asked Scott if he could be considered for the next similar opportunity that came along.

Obviously, not all scenarios will be quite this seamless. When a manager is to review the results with an employee, the employee might well be tempted to improve his or her commitment picture by fudging on the answers. Often, a more effective way to use this instrument is to allow employees to use it and review individual results privately. Even though the manager will not see the results, allowing an employee to self-monitor and self-assess is a powerful step in creating self-motivation. This approach is also consistent with the shared responsibility for commitment that will be a significant focus of this book. Self-assessment and monitoring also build trust, and trust is an essential component for truly effective working relationships in today's work environment.

THE FOUR CORNERSTONES TO COMMITMENT

As you have seen, the Profile examines four areas: vision, insight, acceptance, and integration. These are the four cornerstones of commitment. Here are brief descriptions of each:

Vision, the first step, is the ability to visualize success and anticipate positive results. Without vision, commitment cannot take wing and elevate you to greater heights. Vision provides a detailed picture or blueprint of a goal.

Insight, the second step, is the ability to know yourself and apply this knowledge to your commitment. Our past behavior is an excellent predictor of present and future behavior. We use our experiences to make decisions and they can be an important tool for future success.

Acceptance of the requirements of change, the third step, can prepare us for unexpected setbacks and will help us make healthy adjustments. Committing to new behaviors is often the most difficult part of keeping a commitment.

Integration, the final step, consists of blending your values with your thoughts, words, and actions. This is the true test of commitment.

Each of the next four chapters will explore these four cornerstones of commitment in depth.

The Four Factors of Commitment

- **Vision** . . . create expectations that are realistic, achievable, and have short- and long-term goals.

- **Insight** . . . use your past experiences as a learning tool for future efforts.

- **Acceptance** . . . let go of things you can't control and focus on what you can do.

- **Integration** . . . walk your talk and live your commitment.

3

VISION:
SEEING WHAT CAN BE

VISION: The ability to visualize and anticipate positive results. Without vision, commitment cannot take wing and elevate you to greater heights. Vision provides a detailed picture or blueprint of your goal.

Vision is much more complex than just imagining success. Yet it is such a simple and powerful process that it's amazing more people don't incorporate it into their lives. The objective of this chapter is to help managers fully understand how vision can be used to empower people in a work environment.

Vision is the beginning—literally, the foundation of the process of creating commitment. With vision, a person clearly and specifically sets his sights on a goal. Vision defines the direction to be taken. It provides the ongoing motivation to sustain efforts toward a goal by creating a clear and meaningful mental picture that is realistic and inspiring.

To be effective, envisioning positive results involves both short-term and long-term components and an understanding of the significance of each. Let's take a look at each of these components a little more closely.

▌ TWO DIFFERENT APPROACHES

When we use the power of the mind's eye to envision results, we generally use two different approaches: that of an ultimate end result, and that of a more immediate or smaller goal. The best visioning for a complex or group effort is to continually keep in mind the ultimate goal (long-range visioning), while using easier-to-reach "road stops" (short-term visioning) to work toward it.

This concept reminds me of my work in health promotion. When I was conducting weight-reduction classes, frequently people would enroll in the group mentioning an upcoming class reunion. They would lose weight— then pile the pounds back on after the reunion. The same thing happened just before swimsuit season. People would lose weight temporarily, look great for the summer, then re-accumulate pounds from holiday indulging and inactivity during the winter.

These people were successful at achieving a short-term goal but lost sight of the long-range goal: to keep weight off and enhance their health through permanently changing their lifestyles. I really believe that if more overweight people were able to keep sight of both a short- and long-range vision, a good percentage of the weight-loss centers in the United States would go out of business.

The reverse problem often occurs in corporate settings. Top management defines a large-scale objective related to improved quality or profits, and it is announced and promoted with great fanfare, slogans, and enthusiasm. However, as the objectives are filtered down to the average worker, there is frequently a lack of specific information or definition with regard to how the goal is to be achieved on a day-to-day basis. The end result is that without a short-term vision, workers are left feeling that the company is responsible for the goal, not them. This is clearly not the way to motivate employees to commit to an objective.

In addition, the two approaches, short-term and long-term, motivate people in two different ways. When pursuing a long-term goal, we all appreciate bite-size chunks of success that are achievable and measurable. The newness of each individual effort provides a quick burst of extra energy, so it's easier to maintain momentum while moving toward the ultimate end.

With long-range goals, the rewards are significant and generally fairly obvious. They are the reason(s) the goal was established in the first place. But with the absence of more immediate, measurable success, discouragement can easily set in once the novelty of launching a new effort wears off. Momentum tends to wax and wane, and most people in Western cultures—accustomed to the idea of steady or rapid progression and highly visible achievement—find this disconcerting.

This expectation has historically been supported in business. The long-range career goals of most American workers, particularly in management, have been realized on a more short-term basis via consistent and regular promotions upward through the business hierarchy. However, in today's flatter hierarchies, with the trend toward leaner organizations, the short-range vision of the next promotion and the satisfaction associated with regular successes is no longer a predictable experience. In essence, the primary motivational tool for management has been taken away.

SHARED RESPONSIBILITY

A promotion is significant in a number of ways. In addition to the obvious monetary rewards, there are powerful psychologic motivators as well. Being promoted is a statement that the individual is valued by the company. Being given additional responsibilities is perceived as trust in and respect for the individual's abilities. Increased status is further evidence of importance and worth to the organization. In the absence of this form of recognition, managers are faced with the challenge of helping people to create a new type of vision. People still need to feel valued, trusted, and respected. The key is to create a sense of shared responsibility that is realistic in the context of the 21st century business environment.

For the individual it means learning to refocus expectations to minimize disappointment and frustration. Career paths need to be broader and more comprehensive, incorporating development of more diverse skills and talents. The expectation of being promoted to G6 and popping the champagne to celebrate is a dated form of incentive. *Shifting the focus to accomplishment rather than promotion still allows for celebration and rejoicing.* The long-range vision for the individual is no longer defined as lifetime employment with a particular company and predictable promotions along the way. It is now a career that is stimulating and interesting, with a sense of having made valued contributions. This will require more initiative and responsibility in personal career development and a clear definition of what is satisfying and rewarding. Celebration in 21st century careers will be linked to achieving a "personal best," and honoring performance. It will be more commonplace to see the champagne opened at the completion of a project than for a promotion.

For the manager it means not expecting people to stay on their jobs and perform at high levels just to collect a paycheck. The need for recognition must be attended to regularly. This means a clearer vision of what motivates and excites every individual on the team. It also requires a vision that is more inclusive and not as exclusive or territorial.

For the organization it means creating a vision that incorporates realistic achievable goals that everyone can relate to. It also means rethinking the reward systems that are in place to determine the best methods for recognizing valued contributions instead of defining loyalty in terms of time on the job. Keeping the vision strong requires day-to-day information with regard to how the goal is achieved.

Having stated this, you might be thinking, Okay, so how do we do this? Stating a theory is one thing; implementing it is another thing entirely. The remainder of this chapter will be devoted to the description of visioning strategies for individuals, managers, and organizations.

MENTAL REHEARSAL

Mental rehearsal sends strong internal messages. An important method of using vision is repeatedly and strongly picturing a particular image. This process has been proven to empower individuals to create a potential outcome. Recent research indicates that 85 percent of all track and field athletes in the 1988 Olympics used Visual Motor Behavioral Rehearsal to enhance their performance. Athletes have used this technique for years, visualizing themselves successfully hitting the ball hard with the bat, seeing it go over the fence, or slam-dunking a basketball.

It is more than just a way to "psyche" themselves up. Mental rehearsal has a direct influence on how they perform in the actual game.

There is a powerful psychophysiologic connection between what we visualize and how our bodies respond, and there is an equally important link between our thoughts and our behavior. This isn't intended to imply a guarantee that if you see it you will be it. But vision has a major impact on an individual's belief system and can lay the groundwork either for success or failure.

While working with a midlevel manager in a utilities company I found this technique especially helpful in encouraging successful behavior. Frank had recently assumed responsibility for a new project in an area of business with which he was unfamiliar. He took on the assignment with serious doubts about his ability to succeed. He believed that he had received the assignment by default and was replacing someone who had been eliminated during a recent layoff. He was convinced that his boss put him in charge out of necessity rather than because of his professional competence. Frank envisioned himself failing and the resulting anxiety and stress was, in fact, affecting his performance.

As part of the counseling process, I encouraged him to recognize and challenge these negative expectations and replace them with more practical questions about what would be required to make the project successful. He was able to identify knowledge and abilities he possessed and how they could be generalized to the new arena. He used this insight to identify specific components of the project that he completed successfully. The resulting sense of accomplishment enhanced his confidence and improved his performance on the job. As an added benefit, Frank began to see this as an opportunity to broaden his range of professional experience.

I have also used visualization and mental rehearsal to help people overcome fear of public speaking, anxiety about disciplining employees, and a wide range of stress-related physical ailments such as hypertension, insomnia, and sexual impotence. In using this technique, with physical or stress-related problems, it's important to couple the visualization with relaxation. This can be accomplished by creating a comfortable environment, free of distractions and noise, and taking a few minutes to become calm and centered. When relaxation is associated with visualization of performance in stressful or anxiety-provoking situations, it can facilitate actual attainment of the desired behavior.

▌ TYING VISION TO VALUES

For a vision to have meaning and provide motivation it must be tied to personal values. Many people launch into commitments because they think it's the right thing to do or because someone else is asking them to. Committing to another person's agenda or to satisfy someone else is committing for the wrong reason. To truly make a commitment to work-related objectives, there are questions each of us must ask ourselves:

- How will I benefit personally within the organization's vision?

- What skills and talents do I offer in reaching our organization's vision?

- How do my personal goals relate to the organization's vision?

- Can I contribute significantly to our organizational goals and still feel balanced in my personal life?

- How do I want to see myself as a professional, a manager, and a provider for my family?

Often there is synergy in what is right for the employee and what is right for the organization. The problem is that some individuals don't take the time to integrate the organizational vision with their own vision and get bogged down in the "not invented here" syndrome—as in, this isn't my agenda, it's theirs.

Here's an example of how this tying together process can work. While counseling with a manager in developing a cross-functional team in a manufacturing setting, I was asked to interview one team member who was obviously disengaged from the process. Early in the interview it was apparent to me that this individual had not bought into the team's goals because she felt it was a waste of time and she had more important things to do on her "real" job. She was quite comfortable with her regular job assignments and her team involvement was not something she had asked for.

After spending time exploring and clarifying what she valued and enjoyed about her regular job, we began to identify similarities and mutually satisfying potential in working with the team. Certain things that were important to her, such as meeting deadlines, helping others reach their goals, applying her creativity to novel situations, generating detailed reports and convincing others through highly effective presentations, were also important to the team's success. Her hesitation resulted from the fact that in past team efforts these talents were not utilized and she was frustrated. Through sharing these attributes and expectations with the team members she felt heard and needed. She began to recognize her importance in the process of reaching the team's goals. Her personal needs and the needs of the group matched.

When we incorporate a vision into multiple areas of our lives, it is strengthened and deepened and we are more likely to sustain it. If the commitment enhances self-esteem, there is identity and ownership of the commitment. In the preceding case, self-esteem, issues relating to self-responsibility, relationships, and professional identity were incorporated into the commitment this employee was making to the team.

▌ MANAGEMENT STRATEGIES

It has always been a responsibility of managers to serve as a conduit of sorts, translating organizational objectives and information to departmental and individual functions. As we look at the concept of vision and its role in commitment, this responsibility takes on new significance. The role of managers in communicating and clarifying is essential for individual employees to fully embrace the corporate vision. This is accomplished in two specific ways: clear communication of the requirements and day-to-day behaviors necessary to meet the company's goals, and alignment of individual talents to maximize efficiency and satisfaction.

Many employees don't understand their particular

roles in the organization's vision. The corporate vision of a telecommunications company whose goal is to become a worldwide leader in communication services might be too vague. To the average worker this might as well read: put the first person on Mars. It is nice to know that your company has high ambitions and a will to make things happen. However, with a global statement of this nature, the individual employee is removed from any clear responsibility for accomplishing it. An effective manager will close this gap by developing and communicating clear, specific expectations for participating in the company's goals. This goes beyond the more traditional responsibilities of supervising day-to-day functions. It involves a thorough understanding of corporate values and an effort to make them meaningful at the level of the individual employee.

Another important part of engaging employees is to align individual strengths to the organizational and/or departmental vision. The most effective managers know how to bring out the best in people by having them work on tasks that suit their talents and interests. If you know someone has a real knack for organizing information and working with details and precision, then this person may be the best choice for developing reports and following procedures. Someone else who likes developing new ideas might be best assigned to newer efforts that are less clear and offer a creative challenge.

This ability to identify and appropriately channel individual talent and work styles is essential to inspiring the new corporate loyalty. Employees who are offered opportunities to do what they do well and are recognized for their contributions will respond with dedication to the company and enhanced performance. Specific methods and tools for facilitating this process will be covered in Chapter 7.

ORGANIZATIONAL STRATEGIES

The primary responsibilities related to vision for the organization are to be consistent in communicating the message and to provide the support needed to make the vision a reality. It's one thing to say that your company will be a leader in work and family issues. However, if programs that meet family needs are not supported, such as child care or flexible work arrangements, employees will have no reason to buy into the vision. An organization also has the responsibility to align reward systems with expressed vision. Recognizing individuals and groups that demonstrate behaviors that support or help to meet organizational goals is crucial. The only sure way to reinforce the importance of any stated goal is to reward people for contributing to its success.

Examples of how an organization can keep people focused on key issues and up to date on important information abound. Ford Motor Company does an excellent job of keeping employees informed through TV monitors set up throughout their locations that carry messages from executives, as well as relevant news items. AT&T has a daily electronic mail system that reports on domestic and international information that involves the organization. Other smaller companies hold weekly information meetings to keep people abreast of progress toward organizational goals and to provide a format for employee input and questions.

Key Points in This Chapter

- Create short-term and long-term visions.

- Strive for accomplishment and your personal best.

- Practice visualization techniques to clarify and solidify your vision.

- Be sure your vision is tied to your values.

4

INSIGHT:
SELF-KNOWLEDGE AS POWER

INSIGHT: Self-knowledge and the ability to apply this knowledge to commitment. Our past behavior is an excellent predictor of future behavior. We can use our life experiences to make better decisions and they can be an important tool for future success.

The often repeated maxim that we should learn from our mistakes would save significant time and energy and allow us to avoid numerous setbacks and disappointments if we could just apply it consistently. Past experience provides a valuable perspective that can help us recognize the patterns we have established in life. Any time we seek to improve the quality and strength of our commitment to a company, a project, a relationship, or a new habit, the change will occur in the context of our past experience.

Insight isn't only about mistakes, however; we learn from our successes as well. Commitment is colored by a number of influences including corporate culture, past personal behavior, and our own social culture. Within these contexts, patterns of behaving and interacting tend to establish themselves and become fairly predictable. Insight involves identifying these patterns and defining what works and what doesn't. This information can help us to plan and execute commitments with greater ease and a higher level of satisfaction.

▌ INSIGHT INTO MOTIVATION

Motivation is obviously a very strong factor in determining an individual's level of commitment. Decades ago motivating people at work was a relatively simple endeavor. Power rested at the top of the organization and fear was a powerful inducement to perform. Money served its purpose as well. The radically different lifestyles and faster pace of today's workers have created the need for a more complex "platter of choices" with which to motivate individual employees. The needs of working people are now less directly connected to monetary rewards and are incompatible with a fear-based motivational system. Managers need a comprehensive understanding of human nature and a keen eye for individual differences to determine the best possible tools for motivation.

Motivation, simply stated, is an inner drive that inspires a person to act. A company that is successful at motivating its employees is one that has helped workers to blend their personal goals with those of the organization. In the past, companies accomplished this via *extrinsic* motivators such as salary increases, predictable promotions, or the threat of termination. Today's most effective approaches tap into *intrinsic* motivators.

▌ SIX KEYS TO THE NEW MOTIVATION

To access the powerful energy of intrinsic motivation, a manager must devote time and energy to the following objectives:

1. Create a vision that is clear and specifically involves employees in the process.

2. Communicate the status of the vision often and consistently.

Note: Items 1 and 2 require managers to be honest, supportive, approachable, and fair in dealing with employees. Management must sincerely care about employees and their needs; if not, employees will be aware of it and this will tend to be demotivating. If specific managers have a preference for an authoritarian, detached style, it is wise to offer them the opportunity and coaching to modify it; if they are not willing or able to change, they should have to face consequences for their resistance.

3. Demonstrate a genuine appreciation for employees' efforts. Feeling valued and needed has a powerful and positive impact on the employer/employee bond and it is a major step in winning commitment.

4. Match the skills, interests, and levels of competence each employee possesses to the tasks that are assigned. All of us would like to be able to follow the common advice, find something you love to do, then find someone who will pay you for doing it. This requires initiative on the part of the employee and creative collaboration with the manager.

5. Empower employees to make decisions. Self-managed teams often have astounding success because they are able to work with autonomy and a sense of ownership. The need for independence and control over what we do is inherent in each of us. Providing a work environment that offers these things can work like magic to motivate people.

6. Reward the desired behaviors. Timing is especially important here. Rewards should be offered as soon after the desired behavior as possible. This can be difficult in today's hectic, fast-paced workplace, but it can make the difference between an employee who maintains momentum and one who becomes discouraged.

Developing a leadership style that incorporates these six key factors can be a challenge, particularly for managers who have operated very differently throughout their careers, and it can be virtually impossible in an organization that doesn't support them. Insight into the contemporary worker and what fuels his performance is crucial to winning loyalty and inspiring commitment.

An important point here is that motivation to perform well on the job is not something a manager can *create*, or force to happen. It must be inspired, nurtured, and sustained. The six keys mentioned above are behaviors that have been proven to create an *environment* that encourages motivation and instills commitment. Informed insight into how that kind of environment operates must permeate corporate values and transcend all levels of the organization, from the global vision of the CEO, down to the mind-set of each individual employee. These issues will be discussed in much more detail in subsequent chapters on Organizational Commitment and Building Commitment with Teams.

THE CHANGING VIEW OF MONEY

Since people obviously expect to be paid for their work, it is a logical assumption that money is an effective motivational tool. Some companies still operate on the presumption that paying top-dollar salaries is sufficient to guarantee employee loyalty and sustain outstanding performance. In reality, however, this does not prove to be the case. Many of the major influences on motivation have very little to do with money. People who love their work often say that they would continue to do it, at least in some form, even if they won the lottery or inherited a large sum of money that made them financially independent. Although salary is clearly a necessary and important consideration, as the following statistics indicate, a number of other rewards are powerful influences as well.

A 1993 study conducted by *Industry Week* asked 2,466 workers, What is the biggest long-term motivator for you? The responses were:

- 32.6 percent: Working for a leader with vision and values

- 27.5 percent: Pay raises and bonuses

- 20.7 percent: Being given greater responsibility

- 16.6 percent: Developing the respect of subordinates and peers

- 12.5 percent: Recognition from supervisors

- 8.7 percent: Other

Additional research sheds more light on the subject of money as a motivator:

Herbert Meyer, a pioneer in exploring this issue, reported in the *Harvard Business Review* as early as 1965 that putting the primary focus on money is actually demotivating. An employee may begin to focus on the pay rather than on the task. Also, a wide disparity in salaries among different levels in an organization is not likely to be conducive to teamwork.

Like salaries, promotions are fast becoming less powerful as motivational tools, as organizations flatten and the opportunity to advance is slowed down.

Bonuses can actually function as demotivators when they are tied to a good year for the company or some other global issue that may have had little direct relationship to the individual's performance. If the same employee who received a bonus last year (because the company did well financially) works even harder this year, but a drop in profits dictates that no bonus is forthcoming, it is unlikely that the employee will sustain the same level of motivation in future months.

▌ DIFFERENT STROKES

An additional challenge to managers is developing insight into the varying needs of individual employees. Even though there is a group of basic motivators that tend to work with most people, specific workers may respond better to one type of reinforcement or incentive than to another. A particular member of a work group may need more encouragement and validation while someone else thrives on additional autonomy and control. It requires more time and energy on the part of the manager, but understanding the fine shades of gray in what makes each person tick is crucial to fostering a high level of motivation and inspiring commitment.

Psychologist David McClelland said that there are three relevant work-based needs that differentiate people according to what motivates them:

1. The need for affiliation

2. The need for achievement

3. The need for power

These needs vary in strength and priority depending on the personality and values of the employee.

One tool for gaining insight into how your employees are motivated in the framework of the above-mentioned factors is the Energy Director Assessment System, available through Mosby/Great Performance, Beaverton, Oregon. This system identifies four types of energy: grounding, creative, logic, and relationship. Once individuals identify their particular strengths they are better able to increase energy to meet job stressors and focus their talents accordingly. Participants see their unique talents as important contributions to work and team functioning and this leads to higher performance and motivation.

Other instruments for assessing stress and channeling unique styles to create higher performance include: The Coping Inventory for Stressful Situations (CISS), The Coping Operations Preference Enquiry (COPE), The Coping Resources Inventory (CRI), The Coping Strategies Scales (COSTS), The Job Stress Index (JSI), The Management Burnout Scale, The Occupational Stress Indicator (OSI), The Pikunas Adult Stress Inventory (PASI), The Stress Audit, and the Stress Analysis System.

INDIVIDUAL RESPONSIBILITY

Achieving and maintaining motivation should not be viewed as solely the charge of managers. Each employee has a responsibility to gain insight into what is motivating for him and to seek it out. Even within a work group or an organization that isn't functioning at optimal levels, each of us can take steps to avoid becoming a victim of "environmental inertia" and stay energized. Here are five suggestions for doing this:

1. Embrace positive corporate values. Look for the essential elements of what leaders in the organization deem important and keep them in mind as you make day-to-day decisions.

2. Be clear about your own vision and the necessary requirements for making it a reality.

3. Understand your unique preferences. Seek out tasks that allow you to channel your best talents and skills, and experiment with new or different ways of doing things you don't enjoy as much.

4. Don't be afraid to try something that you don't necessarily have expertise in. Most high achievers broaden their skills and succeed because they are able to overcome the fear of potential failure and give it a shot.

5. Live your personal values. Strive for a healthy and satisfying balance in the work, family, health, community, and spiritual dimensions of your life.

The following tool may prove helpful as well in the process of sustaining energy and momentum.

SELF-MEASURING STICK

List the times or situations in your life when you felt excited and energized about what you were doing. Explore the reasons for your initial excitement and the influences that kept you going. This will help you to identify and evaluate any patterns or similarities. These common themes can provide insight into what motivates you.

Situation	Reason for Initial Excitement	What Kept You Going
Going to school	Self-improvement	Getting good grades
	Anticipating degree	Praise from teachers
Entering a 10K race	Thought of completing the distance	Cheers and applause
		Physical challenge

Use this space to complete your own Self-Measuring Stick:

Situation	Reason for Initial Excitement	What Kept You Going
_____	_____	_____
_____	_____	_____
_____	_____	_____

Once in contact with past experiences that proved to be rewarding and stimulating, you will have a better understanding of what fuels you and how to seek that out in the context of present assignments. Then determine the "have to's" (tasks that offer limited gratification) and think creatively about ways of completing them. Some of the have to's may be more tolerable in a different context; for example, an unexciting monthly report can be done while listening to music or a difficult project might be outlined and formulated while walking or bicycling. Most jobs also include those dreaded tasks that will not be enjoyable or gratifying regardless of the context. They are simply stuff that has to be done. It's wise to schedule these tasks when your energy is highest and discipline yourself to accomplish them on schedule. Getting these unappealing jobs over with will free you up for more meaningful work.

█ UNDERSTANDING PERSONAL HISTORY AND CULTURE

Each of us is a product of our past experiences and the culture in which we have been socialized. The environments we have lived and worked in during the course of our lives shape the way we view the world, the style in which we interact with other people as well as our values and preferences. Much of the work that goes on in psychotherapy involves generating insight into the influences that have fashioned who we are. I have observed how an exploration of personal history provides a flash of awareness, which suddenly makes sense of behaviors and conflicts that have repeatedly caused difficulty for someone. The strength of insight-based therapy is the clarity and logic that can result from this type of awareness. People often express relief when they learn that there are explainable reasons for their dysfunctional behavior. Insight-based therapies also probe the unconscious mind, but this is a long-term and complex process that goes beyond what is advocated here. The insight necessary for sustaining commitments is brought about through a conscious personal exploration of the relationship between what is happening now and what has occurred in the past. In the business setting, the power of insight becomes useful in enhancing commitments to work-related goals and behaviors, particularly as they pertain to our relationships with co-workers. An understanding of the role of culture in shaping behavior, for example, is crucial for appreciating diversity and minimizing misunderstandings between people who work together. People who were socialized in very dissimilar cultures often misinterpret each other's comments and behavior, and sometimes we can come across different from what we intend when the person we are interacting with has a history unlike our own. To maximize the benefits of diversity in today's work setting, it is necessary to have insight into these issues.

I facilitated a series of team-building seminars for a mail-order catalog company and Robert, who managed the information systems group, illustrates this point. He had been struggling for almost a year to bring together a team of computer programmers who had been functioning with a great deal of individual autonomy prior to his being assigned as their manager. The previous manager had pretty much let people set their own goals and determine their own priorities based on project requests from other departments. When Robert joined the organization, he was asked to help the group develop a more unified vision and a team approach to getting the job done. His subordinates were resistant and had complained about the fact that he was too controlling and authoritarian. They resented his requests to be appraised of what they were doing on a daily basis and felt that he made decisions without considering their input. During an exercise that involved sharing information about each individual's personal history, Robert related that both his parents were Italian immigrants and that he was the oldest of four children. He described his father as a man who commanded loyalty and respect, and spoke for several minutes about his value for family and children and his appreciation for openly expressed emotion and a sense of fun. During the feedback session, members of the team expressed the frustrations described above, but also thanked Robert for his humor, his high energy level, and his sensitivity when it came to family issues. They acknowledged that it was very helpful to know that they could leave early to accommodate a day-care problem, or adjust their schedules for pediatricians' appointments and school functions. I saw clearly (especially since his culture was very familiar to me) that Robert's family of origin had shaped both the behaviors that were working for him and those that weren't. In my experience, men in Mediterranean cultures are typically socialized to take charge and to exercise control. Their style of communication is very direct and straightforward and when they are in a position of authority, they are expected to know the right thing to do and to see that it gets done. Usually, the culture is also very child and family centered and places a high value on laughter and enjoying life. When we discussed these influences on Robert's behavior, two things happened. The group gained insight into the meaning behind their manager's actions and recognized that he wasn't really as authoritarian as he was coming across, and Robert recognized how a style of communicating and taking charge that came naturally to him was preventing him from reaching his goals. Everyone involved now had information that they could use to improve the way they worked together.

Not only the cultures we are raised in, but those of the organizations we have worked in can shape our expectations, behavior, and values. I once consulted with a supervisor who had recently begun working for a software company after spending 20 years in the Navy. He was experiencing a great deal of stress at work, and it was due primarily to significant differences between the organizational cultures of the armed forces and the private sector. During his naval career, Joe had become accustomed to functioning within very specific guidelines and performing according to precisely outlined procedures. He was also used to a direct chain-of-command reporting structure. The company where he was currently employed had an informal atmosphere and utilized a matrix management process. Much of the work was creative and somewhat abstract in nature, and Joe described himself as feeling like a fish out of water. Even the relaxed style of dress that was the norm at this company felt somewhat foreign to him. In addition to this, Joe's co-workers had expressed irritation with his tendency to obsess over relatively unimportant details. They resented his tendency to become angry when someone who reported to him completed a task in a different way from what he had suggested. Joe was perceived by others as uptight and rigid. By evaluating his work history, and discussing it with some of the key people he worked with, Joe was able to recognize the source of his conflict and stress and to begin adapting his work style to the new environment. Once co-workers had some insight into his behavior, they were more tolerant of it. They teased him about his precision and even jokingly referred to him as "Captain" or "sir."

Insights such as those described above serve to strengthen both individual and team commitments. An understanding of where we have come from and an appreciation and respect for the life experiences and values of others allow us to reinforce and build on the human element of work.

ACTING ON INSIGHT

Insight, as I have described it thus far, provides a lifetime perspective through which the individual learns about motivators, cultural influences, and personal characteristics—essentially an inventory of one's life. Acting on this information is another task entirely, and as both research and personal experience tell us, a much greater challenge in maintaining commitments. If *knowing* was easily translated into *doing*, most counselors, psychologists, trainers, and coaches would be out of business, and self-help methodologies would provide the answers everyone is looking for. Knowledge is worth little unless it is utilized.

One of the most important ways of integrating insights into action is in the defining and modifying of our lifestyles. An illustration of this process is in the area of health commitments. Many people suffering from heart disease are informed and educated about the detrimental effects of their high-fat diets and sedentary, stressful way of living. To take full advantage of this information requires not just a knowledge of how cholesterol clogs arteries, but specific and viable methods for consistently consuming less of it at meals. For an individual whose family culture advocates a bacon and eggs breakfast and well-marbled steak as part of the ideal dinner, significant modifications in meal planning are "where the rubber meets the road." I have found in treating depressed patients that while insight into the historical, environmental, or biochemical causes of their illness is helpful, it is changes in the way they live their lives that actually make the greatest difference. For example, factors such as meaningful work, supportive relationships, and regular exercise have often proved to be as effective as medication in counteracting this disorder (Lazarus, 1981).

The same principle holds true for work-related commitments. I have heard many young employees describe the adjustments that were required in making the transition from college life to a full-time job. Late nights out and frequent socializing can make it difficult to be sharp and fresh at an 8 AM meeting. Often a modification in lifestyle is necessary for these individuals to sustain commitments to team and personal career goals. The greatest challenge in adhering to work commitments is balancing our personal lives with the demands of our jobs. Navigating the complex set of issues involved in this endeavor will be necessary for defining the lifestyles of the 21st century worker.

Using insight in an organization to change the norms of the culture creates an atmosphere that is conducive to optimal performance. Attempting to sustain commitments in a culture that doesn't support your efforts is like swimming upstream. Not only does it require twice the energy, but it's also tempting to give in and end the battle. Insight into the prevailing norms of your work, family, and social culture will help to assess potential setbacks as well as sources of support. This doesn't have to be a formal assessment (see discussion of culture audits in Chapter 7), but merely a review of the people and practices that can encourage you or get in your way.

Think about what it is that you are committing to. If it's a personal commitment, such as caring for an elderly parent, think about how the culture supports your efforts or hinders them. For instance, there may be home care services available in your community (support), or you may feel the pressure from relatives to provide care in your home, because that's the way it has always been done in your family. Obviously, you will want to turn to supports for assistance. However, you will also want to know when sustaining your motivation will be more difficult because of resistance or interference.

I have learned that it is futile to conduct stress management seminars unless they are offered as part of a comprehensive organizational commitment to reduce unwanted stress. Too frequently these types of programs are requested to treat the symptom and not the underlying ill-ness. Corporate cultures that continue to treat people as disposable resources (bring them in, burn them out, and replace them) and offer stress management as a bandaid, will continue to suffer the ill effects of stress despite the best short-term remedies. A more effective approach is to offer stress management as an *adjunct* to a more global ini-tiative of reducing unnecessary stress in the system. Learning skills to manage stress then becomes part of an organizational plan to attend to the needs of employees while creating a healthier work environment.

In summary, the role of insight in commitment is to as-sist us in fine-tuning our visions. Self-knowledge can help us to avoid setbacks, create realistic expectations, and ac-knowledge the value of our past experience. When it is applied to daily living, the result is a lifestyle in which commitments can flourish.

Key Points in This Chapter

- Review life experiences and identify patterns of behavior.

- Identify what motivates you and your employ-ees.

- Assume responsibility for sustaining motiva-tion.

- Evaluate the influence of personal history and culture on behavior, perceptions, values and communication.

5

ACCEPTANCE:
THE EMOTION ELEMENT

ACCEPTANCE of the requirements of change is necessary and is the third step toward commitment. Acceptance of these requirements can prepare us for unexpected setbacks and will help us make healthy adjustments. Committing to *doing things differently* is often the most difficult part of keeping a commitment.

Commitment and change are inextricably linked together. Adapting to any major change successfully requires commitment, and any new commitment involves change. It is human nature to resist change. Significant change involves a loss of the familiar. It creates uncertainty and ambiguity, as well as a disruption of existing activities and feelings. Most people become uncomfortable and even anxious under these conditions.

Because resistance is a natural part of the process of change, managers need to expect it and be prepared to handle it. The purpose of this chapter is to address the way people work through resistance. Using the word AC-CEPT as an acronym, we will explore six psychologic tasks necessary for the transition from resistance to commitment:

- Awareness. Understanding the personal impact of change and individual emotional responses.

- Control. Channeling energy in appropriate ways and fostering personal accountability.

- Choice. Translating accountability to "in the moment" thoughts and behaviors.

- Efficacy. A sense of empowerment and a belief in positive outcome.

- People. Creating reciprocal nurturing and support. Involving others in your commitment.

- Troubleshooting. Anticipating and planning for obstacles. Let's take a more in-depth look at each of these tasks.

AWARENESS

Imagine going on a group business trip that will last for an indefinite period. It will disrupt your already busy, demanding schedule. Now imagine that you are not sure where you are going or how you will get there. Once you arrive at your destination, there is no clear direction about what you're trying to accomplish. In addition, the trip is not something you have expressed interest in and you had no say in deciding to make the excursion in the first place.

What is your reaction? What would be your level of cooperation, involvement, and support for others going with you?

Unfortunately, for many people in today's business environment, this is very much what it feels like when significant organizational changes are made. Not only are the reasons for change not clearly communicated, but the impact and involvement of the employees in navigating the change are indefinite as well. This leaves many people feeling not only confused, but unimportant, resentful, and bitter.

Many managers assume that employees will understand that change is part of doing business and that employees' loyalty to business objectives should transcend any temporary confusion or discomfort. Actually, there is a somewhat valid basis for that assumption. Most of us experience initial resistance and confusion, but as time passes we adjust to changes and incorporate them into our daily routines.

However, this process happens much more smoothly *when we have an understanding of the personal impact of the change and a sense of control about it.* A skilled manager can significantly shorten the time between initial resistance and acceptance by attending to this valid need for information. Organizational change magnifies the responsibility for clear and ongoing communication on all levels.

When organizational change is major, such as in a merger or downsizing, the need for information is even more imperative. Many companies lose talented workers because personally relevant information wasn't communicated at crucial times during downsizing. Because their value wasn't expressed explicitly, many high-performance employees take early retirement or departure packages when offered to the company at large. Some companies have learned to be more strategic in their efforts to keep key individuals. They have learned that people need reassurance and direction in turbulent times. Experience has also taught them that rumors will quickly fill the gap created by an absence of real information. Failure to counteract this process not only deteriorates morale but also takes its toll in loss of productivity as people waste time and energy in speculation and are less motivated to complete tasks.

▌ EMOTIONAL BARRIERS

Awareness of *emotional barriers* to change is an important step in the transition through acceptance to commitment. There are hosts of emotional reactions when dealing with major change. Even with changes that are expected and welcome, such as having a child, there are psychologic responses that can be difficult to work through. These responses can interfere with a full and rewarding commitment. (The vast number of magazine articles and books to help new parents adjust attest to this.) When the change is *not* welcome and/or occurs unexpectedly—as is often the case with organizational change—individual psychologic responses can be complex and painful enough to stand in the way of effective adjustment.

To prevent emotions from becoming barriers, three psychologic tasks (listed below as steps 1–3) must be completed.

STEP 1

Recognize that any significant change will elicit emotional reactions and that these feelings, if not managed appropriately, can interfere with commitment. This step involves expecting to have feelings about a significant change, and identifying what those feelings are. Although this might sound simple, many of us don't have much day-to-day experience in "naming" our emotions. We might even be reluctant to do so, especially if the feelings are unpleasant ones. Furthermore, the traditional business environment hasn't been interested in or supportive of the expression of human emotions. Many people have been strongly encouraged *not* to express emotion in the workplace. Keeping this in mind, many people have found it helpful to use the following list of "feeling" words to clarify their emotional responses to change:

Anger	Frustration	Resentment
Hostility	Aggravation	Anxiety
Insecurity	Self-doubt	Fear
Tension	Sadness	Grief
Sense of loss	Depression	Discouragement
Confusion	Uncertainty	Embarrassment
Guilt	Excitement	Anticipation
Gratitude	Relief	Sense of challenge

This is a short list of some possible responses. It might be helpful for a manager to create a comprehensive list, especially as it applies personally.

When emotions go unrecognized, they have a way of coming back to haunt us later as stress, strained relationships, and even illness.

STEP 2

Express your feelings in appropriate ways that will enable you to be heard, and to have your personal needs met. People vary in terms of what they need when they are faced with the task of working through significant feelings. For some people, a supportive, listening ear is sufficient. They need to be heard and to think out loud to clarify and process their emotions. Many of us find validation of our feelings very helpful, too. When respected friends or co-workers tells us that they understand our experience, they validate our emotions and it's a relief for us. Hearing that others share our feelings is often reassuring as well.

But many people prefer not to discuss their feelings in detail, if at all. Their most helpful strategy is to identify and work through the emotions privately by writing them down or simply thinking introspectively. They can then use interpersonal supports in more of a problem-solving or practical context.

The task here is for each of us to determine what type of outlet (conversation, group meetings, journaling, introspective thinking, etc.) is most likely to be helpful, and then to identify and utilize it. Just remember, the important thing is *not to ignore or de-emphasize* significant feelings.

STEP 3

Re-evaluate the importance of the commitment, and if a decision is made to remain committed, understand how continuing to focus on negative emotions can get in the way of success.

Once emotions have been identified and addressed appropriately, another look at the commitment itself is in order. There are situations in which the emotions associated with a particular goal or objective are so profound that they need to be listened to. Emotions contain valid and important messages about what is important to us and what we need and want out of life.

Occasionally in marriage counseling, I have worked with couples who, after confronting and processing their respective feelings, determine that the relationship is no longer viable; that each of them is unhappy enough or their unmet needs significant enough that they would be wiser to separate.

Some commitments simply aren't worth the price we have to pay emotionally to maintain them. In a business context, there are some changes that create an intolerable work environment or conditions of employment. If this is the case, it is not only appropriate, but responsible to pursue alternate job options.

If it is determined that the commitment is worth maintaining, it is important to be aware of how negative emotions can impede progress toward a goal. This is really a question of focus and will be addressed in more detail in the upcoming section on Choice. The initial task is to recognize that feelings can slow down and even prevent adaptation to new situations.

If emotional barriers are not *recognized* or anticipated, performance may be hindered. Providing opportunities for this emotional awareness is a responsibility of both the individual and the manager. Although some people might perceive inquiry into feelings by the manager as an invasion of privacy, it is possible to convey care and understanding without being intrusive.

MANAGERIAL RELUCTANCE

It has been my experience that many managers are somewhat reluctant to involve themselves in the realm of their employees' emotions. This is due in part to a lack of familiarity with psychological matters. Most managers haven't been trained as psychologists, and don't want to be. Furthermore, while managers are often hired based on their ability to lead, those who have strong leadership skills often have strong, take-charge personalities. It has been my experience that these more forceful, task-oriented people tend to prefer the more tangible and practical to the nebulous arena of human emotions. This may or may not be true for any given manager, but I want to be very clear that I don't suggest that managers offer any form of counseling or psychotherapy; rather, they are responsible for supporting a context in which the awareness can occur. A skilled manager is able to communicate, at least in general terms, that emotional responses to change are normal and expected and will be addressed. The skills needed to do this are simple and concrete. Frequently a carefully worded statement or two, offering validation and support, can lay the groundwork for positive change.

Providing people with an opportunity to express and

acknowledge their feelings is often best facilitated by an outside professional trained in group facilitation or organizational psychology. The group setting is ideal, since it not only allows freedom of expression but also provides an opportunity for the kind of validation and support described earlier. Even people who are reluctant to say what is on their minds might be encouraged when they hear that others think and feel as they do. Depending on the nature of the change, the group process might be more effective if the manager is *not* present.

A Midwestern telephone company asked me to conduct seminars on dealing with change as part of their major downsizing efforts. An integral part of these seminars were group sessions allowing employees to express how they felt about the changes. Initially, there was hesitation, then as some individuals began to speak up, more people chimed in. After a couple of hours, there was a sense of relief and appreciation. A number of employees approached me after the sessions saying that the process was extremely helpful for them. They liked expressing their feelings and felt understood by others in the process. I heard such statements as, "It's great to know I'm not the only one who feels this way" and "I wasn't sure exactly how I felt until I had a chance to discuss it."

The manager of the group acknowledged a change in the climate at work. Even though there was pain later as a result of the anticipated layoffs, those affected seemed much better able to accept the changes.

This type of approach may be useful for companies concerned about workplace violence as well.

It should be made clear, though, that the sessions with

the telephone company worked because it was a very *structured, professionally directed, and time-limited* psychological intervention. Managers can attest to the negative, destructive influence of "gripe groups" that exist informally in most workplaces. Managers don't need to arrange or encourage "bitch sessions" in the work environment. This is not only unproductive but may well serve to reinforce the types of emotional barriers to adjustment discussed in this section.

CONTROL

The role of control in relation to stress is clear. People who have a perception of control tend to deal with stress more effectively. This is mostly due to a sense that they can predict the outcome of their actions and are not subject to the whims of someone else. Classic studies have shown that people and animals put into stressful situations and deprived of a sense of control experience adverse physical and emotional symptoms (Sutherland, J.E., 1991). Also, research with managers has shown control to be a hardiness factor that can mitigate the harmful effects of stress (Maddi, S., and Kobasa, 1984).

But how is it measured? How much of a sense of control does an individual need to make lasting and meaningful commitments? To understand this, we need to recognize that there are in fact definite and definable variations in personality that determine need for direction and the degree of control needed.

There is a lot of truth in the old belief that some people are leaders and some are followers. There is also a variation in the control needs of leaders and followers. Leaders seek and demand control because it fits with their approach to solving problems and getting things done. They tend to be more *internal* in their locus of control, which means they are more likely to operate out of the belief that the way to get things done is to do them yourself. In stressful situations they are not content to wait and see what happens or to depend on others to take action. They are looking for ways to influence the change process.

Followers are more *external* in their locus of control. They will seek solutions outside of themselves to resolve problems. This is particularly relevant to commitments, since leaders will more likely respond to change with self-initiative and followers will probably need more support and encouragement.

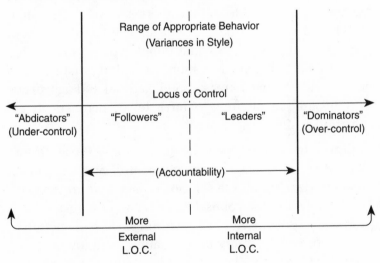

Control can be abused and disruptive. Certain individuals (dominators) use control to bolster their self-esteem and to try to create a sense of omnipotence. These people not only hurt themselves, frequently developing ulcers, tension headaches, and hypertension, but they also tend to alienate and overwhelm others.

DREADED FRED

While working with a quality improvement team, the issue of control surfaced as a major stumbling block. The team leader, Fred, was someone who inflicted his authority and need for control on just about everyone he worked with. He rarely took time to hear what others had to say on how the group could reach its goals—if he even allowed them to express their opinions. Fred had a pattern of responding with hostility to any attempt by another member of the team to initiate an idea without clearing it with him first. The group became stagnant and the lack of progress only served to make things worse. Frustration caused Fred to behave in a more controlling manner than before. He became increasingly dictatorial and aggressive in a misguided attempt to force team members to get something done.

Opposite the Fred type, the dominator, is the abdicator. Abdicators refuse to assume any control and depend on others to develop all the solutions. Jack was an example. He came to me for counseling because of a relationship problem. His girlfriend had told him she'd had enough of his lack of responsibility in maintaining employment and his procrastination. Jack was full of complaints and excuses. He claimed that one employer didn't give him enough time to get things done, another didn't recognize his skills, and so on. In listening to Jack, it was obvious that he was overly dependent on everyone in his life to accommodate him and was also oblivious to his patterns of behavior. He was, however, willing to attempt to change since the relationship was important to him and he did want to maintain stable employment.

These two polar opposites show how individuals address the issue of control and the negative effects that these extremes can produce. Somewhere in between domination and abdication lies a healthy balance of control, called *accountability*.

Accountability and self-responsibility go hand in hand and are vital to the establishment and maintenance of commitments. In Jack's case he not only was unable to keep a steady job; he also had difficulty maintaining a meaningful relationship. His victimized thinking was a major drain on his self-esteem. It often resulted in his giving up or abandoning commitments. Fred's difficulties were centered on his lack of accountability to others and his disregard for their role in *mutual* commitments.

The key to achieving a healthy balance of accountability lies in an individual's ability to discriminate between what he is in charge of and what he is not. Anyone familiar with the Serenity Prayer has thought about the importance of "accepting things that cannot be changed, having the courage to change the things that can, and the wisdom to know the difference." Accountability is the wisdom to know the difference.

CHOICE

Once we decide on a direction to take, how do we stay focused and change behaviors that have developed over the years? These become deeply ingrained and can be difficult to break. The answer is "in the moment" thinking—a way of changing automatic responses into deliberate self-statements of self-responsibility. I call this technique full-choice thinking. It is a cognitive process based on focus. It includes letting go of the emotions interfering with your commitment and making the most of the decision you have made. Full-choice thinking is based on the idea that our thoughts determine how we feel about things, and thus we create predictable patterns of behavior based on those thoughts. It is also one of the most powerful methods for changing nonproductive habits and weak commitments.

Several years ago I was offered a career advancement with a Fortune 100 company for whom I worked. This opportunity required me to move to the East from the Midwest, where I also had a thriving private practice, as well as family and friends. It was an opportunity to work at the company's world headquarters and be in a greater position of influence and involvement. My thoughts took the following forms:

1.   Questioning the need for the move: I can do this job from my present location. Why do I have to move?

2.   Anticipating negative outcomes: What if I get there and come under the control of an overly demanding manager?

3.   Feeling guilty: My family will be disrupted—besides, they might hate the East Coast.

I was stuck in the half-choice mode. I had decided to take the job, but had not focused on the thoughts that would help me make the most of my decision. This awareness enabled me to refocus and turn my attention in a more positive direction. I began to think not of *losing* my private practice, but of relocating it. I anticipated summers spent at the beach, which I loved. I also anticipated reconnection with my family of origin in the East and saw it as a way to rekindle family ties and even make new friends. This change in focus led to new emotions (anticipation, excitement) and less resentment, fear, and guilt. I had made a full choice. I had aligned my thoughts with my decision.

Full-choice thinking is essential for successful commitments in life or at work. This technique is helpful in making major commitments, such as a move, or can be useful in minimizing the emotional drain in day-to-day decisions. Full-choice thinking involves:

1. Deciding on the best choice at that time. A decision is required. (I could have turned down the promotion.)

2. Once the decision is made, focusing your thoughts on the positive benefits of the choice. Remember, *ownership* of a decision allows for release of any anger or resentment in carrying it out.

EFFICACY

A major reason people get stuck in resistance is that they don't really believe there is anything they can do about a situation. Even if they did take action to change things they think they wouldn't be any better off. Most of the time this is an unconscious process.

Albert Bandura, a pioneer in cognitive psychology,

identifies self-efficacy as a belief in one's ability to influence and direct a particular situation and an expectation of a positive outcome in doing so. This two-part belief has been used by psychologists and health care workers to help people change habits and behaviors that are unhealthy or counterproductive.

In the business setting, it is embodied in empowerment initiatives. The problem with some attempts at empowerment is that managers think that simply giving someone authority or permission to make decisions is sufficient. For those people with a more internal locus of control, mentioned earlier, it might be enough. However, followers might need a stronger belief in their own abilities and a more powerful expectation of a positive outcome. The commitment it takes for someone to assume responsibility (empowerment) must incorporate this key belief system.

A manager can facilitate empowerment through a variety of simple techniques and exercises. The following is an activity form I have used with a wide range of groups, addressing topics from addiction to downsizing to weight management. It helps the participant build confidence and self-efficacy by remembering successful prior attempts to overcome difficulties. This information can be generalized to help fuel new commitments.

My Personal History of Effective Commitments

A difficult change and commitment I experienced: _____

_____

Once I decided to do it, I: _____

_____

In order to be successful, I had to: _____

_____

Once I reached my goal, I felt better about myself because: _____

_____

What I learned about myself in keeping this commitment was: _____

_____

Virtually every person has at some point had to deal with difficult changes and has struggled with a major commitment of some sort. By recalling these times when we have been tested and overcome resistance, we can tap into our unique strengths and coping styles. We then begin to assess ourselves as capable of overcoming barriers and obstacles—whether they are self-imposed barriers or resistance from others in our lives. This activity also prepares the individual for potential problems and setbacks since much of the resistance we experience follows a repeated pattern.

▎ LOIS'S STORY

Much of the courage it takes to do something is achieved by recognizing the courage of having done it before. Some people draw on past personal experiences to deal with difficult work-related changes. Lois, a participant in a managing change workshop, was having significant difficulty addressing the potential loss of her job in an upcoming downsizing. She was aware of her anger toward the company but was reluctant to address her feelings. She repeatedly verbalized her hope that she would be retained in her position due to her long years and good record with the company. She was resistant to participating in the exercises I introduced that involved thinking ahead to what it would be like to leave the company or what options existed for her beyond her current job.

When I asked the group (which included Lois) to complete the above form, she appeared to be thinking intently about it. She spent a great deal of time on her answers. When a group discussion was initiated, Lois surprised me by volunteering to share her responses. She began by saying she hadn't realized how frightening the potential layoff was to her. Apparently this was her first and only corporate position and she believed that her skills might not translate themselves well to a job in another company.

I had introduced the exercise by saying that everyone in the room had at some point faced a significant and difficult change and survived. I asked them to identify such a change and then respond to the questions. Lois shared that she had at one time been involved in an abusive marriage to an alcoholic and had found the courage to leave with her two small children, find employment, and make a life for herself as a single mother. She had realized in a way that she did possess the strengths and skills necessary to confront a new and uncertain future. "I'm a survivor," she declared, a determined expression on her face.

PEOPLE

No commitment exists in a vacuum. With any meaningful commitment we make, there are people who are affected by it and directly involved in it. Understanding the impact of these important people and the roles they play in our commitments is a key factor in overcoming resistance and gaining essential support.

First, we need to be aware of the ways people sabotage our efforts and work against us. Much of the time I spent as a rehabilitation counselor was in helping drug addicts deal with the destructive influence of their peers. Getting people off drugs was minor compared to the task of establishing a support system where there were not others constantly tempting them with drugs and sabotaging their abstinence.

The same holds true for other commitments. Other people don't always have our best interests in mind, even when they express the importance of our commitments. For a variety of reasons they might not want to see us succeed or might question the wisdom of our decisions. Because we care about important people, we don't want to offend them or hurt the relationship. Therefore, we allow them to interfere with our commitments, or we're reluctant to ask for their help and support. In fact, sometimes we go to extremes to protect ourselves and others.

We have heard about the terminated manager who postpones telling his family that he has lost his job and for weeks gets dressed in the morning and drives around all day, pretending to be at work. I have worked with managers who were reluctant to break the bad news to a work group, deliberately withholding information that could have helped others make important career decisions. The fact is, we rely on others for support and encouragement and others rely on us for honesty and reassurance. The PEOPLE part of acceptance is being aware of how others influence and affect you and how your commitment affects them. From a management perspective, this means understanding the interpersonal dynamics of the people who work for you and what you can do to inform and support them.

It's important to look at this issue from two perspectives: (1) What do people need from me? and (2) What do I need from them?

As with communicating vision, the manager's role in

supporting commitments primarily involves providing accurate and timely information and communicating concern in a sincere manner. There are three specific ways in which managers fall short of their responsibility toward people in the context of change: enabling behaviors, withholding information, and inflexible management styles.

1. *Enabling behaviors* often take the form of consciously and/or unconsciously protecting someone by turning your back on dysfunctional behaviors or allowing disruptive activities to occur. Enabling takes many forms, from giving someone satisfactory performance ratings when their performance is unsatisfactory to ignoring behaviors that disrupt team performance (such as open criticism of team members that is malicious and damaging).

Enabling sends the same message, no matter which way it's used: You can continue to do these things and get away with it. This is not only destructive for the person being enabled (preventing that person from growing and learning as a result of the experience), but it can hurt a manager's credibility. Helping people keep their work-related commitments requires honest feedback—and at times, confrontation. For most enabling managers, this is very hard to do. They might not feel it's their business or might assume that the subordinate will figure it out. There is also a good deal of discomfort involved in confronting someone; enablers avoid anything that resembles interpersonal conflict. In conflict situations, honesty can be both painful and freeing, but it might require that the manager put significant energy into altering his or her behavior.

2. *Withholding information* is deliberately keeping relevant and important information from people who need it.

Why do managers do this? Well, part of the reason is similar to why enabling behaviors take place: to avoid discomfort. Another reason might be to exercise control and authority. This is a more abusive version of withholding and requires a more thorough look into the motivations of the manager.

3. *Inflexible management styles* do not meet the various needs of subordinates and peers. Much has been written on this subject and most managers know the differences in various approaches to management style. To support commitments, the style of management required depends on the particular employee and on the issue involved. More of this will be covered in the next chapter.

▌ TROUBLESHOOTING

The final step in overcoming resistance through acceptance is troubleshooting for possible setbacks and planning for them. The treatment of addictive behaviors often includes a strategy called *relapse prevention.* Controlling an addiction is such a long-term (often life-long) process that intermittent progress requires extensive focus. Relapse prevention helps patients reframe any lapse or deviation as a learning process, rather than a complete relapse. The magnitude of the lapse loses its totality. This helps the person battling addiction to bypass the idea, "I slipped so I might as well start drinking again," and adapt the thought, "I realize how this particular instance happened, so I can prevent it from happening in that particular way again."

This psychological principle can have great impact in the business world to help inspire commitment. Applying the strategy to the workplace involves backing up the process and anticipating the things that start it in motion. It requires identifying the thoughts, emotions, behaviors, and environmental factors that influence commitment. This is crucial in *keeping* commitments, since many well-intended commitments falter when the old patterns surface in response to old triggers.

The savvy manager is aware of the repetitive cycles that occur and their effect on people. For instance, there are certain times of the year when deadlines have to be met, budgets are lean, or work is slow. People react in certain ways to these cycles and managers need to anticipate this. Skill is required to use this information to facilitate commitments of all employees; it's more than effective time and resource management, and includes a strategic approach to channeling the emotional energy of people.

There are also certain individuals who tend to create trouble repeatedly. Any well-planned group effort that requires commitments from everyone will include a strategy for dealing with attitudes and behaviors that can infect others, such as complaints, negativity, etc. A sure way to destroy the energy of a high-performing group is to allow negative people to run amuck.

Troubleshooting is often thought of as putting out fires, but in sustaining commitment from employees, troubleshooting needs to be thought of as a preventive tool. It can be an effective means of avoiding potential setbacks, but it requires a process of ongoing feedback and checking in on the progress and status of commitment goals. This process is best carried out in an informal and timely manner.

Key Points in This Chapter

- Work through resistance with ACCEPT: Awareness, Control, Choice, Efficacy, People, and Troubleshooting.

- Accountability and self-responsibility go hand in hand and are vital to the establishment and maintenance of commitments.

- Full-choice thinking is the most efficient way to bolster decisions you have made.

6

INTEGRATION:
THE DEMONSTRATION OF COMMITMENT

INTEGRATION means blending your values with your thoughts, words, and actions. This is the true test of commitment.

We have progressed through three important stages of commitment:

- Vision, the beginning point of any significant commitment

- Insight, where we learn about ourselves and the patterns of behavior we need to be aware of

- Acceptance, a key factor in managing our emotional response to change

This chapter focuses on the final and most important of the four factors of commitment: Integration. Integration is the blending of our *thinking, verbalizations,* and *behaviors* that are necessary to maintain commitment.

Commitment doesn't mean just following through on a promise or fulfilling an obligation. A true commitment is maintained consistently and with passion. It is not only a matter of the mind but also of the heart. In this respect, commitment must arise out of and be related to the things

most important to us. When this happens, we are integrated.

Many commitments require the faith to venture forward to make sacrifices and confront the unknown. A
person who cares deeply about a commitment is more
likely to be successful in sustaining it. One reason that
many commitments falter is that people invest themselves
halfheartedly or temporarily in something that doesn't
have real meaning for them. It is fairly easy to generate a
short-term burst of enthusiasm for a new idea or trend.
The newest flavor of the month in any workplace will at-
tract a host of eager supporters. However, as the newness
wears off, so does the enthusiasm. Most managers have
had experience with this pattern but are compelled to respond to the latest trends as well. The importance of integration in commitment is based on the fact that when we
demonstrate inconsistencies in what we think, say, and do,
we confuse others and send internal messages to ourselves
of lack of conviction and interest.

A major challenge for today's manager is to maintain
momentum for a sufficient period to accomplish the goals
that have been established. People need to be committed
to a work ethic that is personal and meaningful. In the
business world, which is in constant flux, the only realistic
commitment is to doing a job well and finding satisfaction
in it.

Integration is particularly important to business-related
commitments, especially when customers are involved.
Inconsistencies in customer service can be deadly, resulting in lost business and confidence. Customers today are
savvy and demanding, due in part to the numerous quality and customer relations programs available to business.

These efforts have established expectations of sensitivity, responsiveness, and respect. When people say one thing and do another, or follow through on a customer's request begrudgingly, it projects a message of indifference that will not be tolerated. Customers are also sensitive to negative comments about the company or work environment and will often equate the quality of the company with the product or service.

Even when our commitments are truly sincere, sometimes we unconsciously sabotage them. On occasion we are all prone to inconsistencies in commitment behaviors that are usually based in the way we think.

My past 20 years of experience as a consultant, manager in a Fortune 500 company, and private-practice psychologist have convinced me that a person's state of mind determines his or her emotions, impacts the physiological state, and strongly influences behavior. This frame of reference has also been articulated by internationally known psychologists presenting cognitive-based theories of human behavior. According to cognitive psychologists, how a person thinks determines mood or emotions, and consequent behaviors.

One such theorist is Albert Ellis, who contends that one's thinking and emotions operate in a circular fashion: the thinking leads to emotions, and the resulting emotions create thoughts. Ellis also believes that people have an inherent capacity to act in either a healthy or productive manner or in nonproductive and unhealthy ways, and that these behaviors are driven by "rational" or "irrational" thoughts. The goal of Ellis's brand of therapy, Rational Emotive Therapy, is to change the maladaptive behaviors by challenging the person's irrational thoughts. Once the person becomes aware of these irrational thoughts and the resulting behaviors, he is encouraged to replace them with more rational ways of thinking.

For instance, in my private practice I've seen many people who catastrophize. When things do not turn out as an individual expects, the resulting thought can be, This is a major catastrophe. Such thinking creates feelings of anger and extreme frustration. The subject matter can vary. Frank sees his job loss as the end of the world. Bob views his marital breakup as a factor that will keep him from ever being happy again. Jane perceives the problems derived from her juvenile-delinquent son as the catalyst to bankrupt her financially and emotionally.

The goal in such situations is to replace the thoughts with a less extreme, more realistic view. A more appropriate thought would be, This is unpleasant and bothersome, but I can let go of the things I can't control and not catastrophize over these disappointments.

Ellis's thinking approach to changing behavior has influenced many other psychologists, counselors, and behavior change experts. His work has also influenced many training programs in business and organizational effectiveness.

The basis for many of these approaches is that our thinking can propel us forward or set us back, depending on the nature of the thoughts and emotions that follow. When our thoughts are positive, our mood is as well. We are more likely to behave in positive ways. When our thoughts are negative and our expectations low, we can anticipate behaving negatively. Integration begins with thoughts that help to create and advance our intended commitment.

There are certain thoughts, however, that will do just the opposite. These thoughts fall into four disruptive styles of thinking and they can be counted on to prevent successful commitments. The styles are:

- Denial

- Discouragement

- Oppositional thinking

- Externalized thinking

These thinking styles can cause breakdowns in the mental, verbal, and behavioral components of integration. Let's take a closer look at each.

DENIAL

Denial is more than being impervious to a situation or event. It is an ongoing lack of responsibility. People in denial have myriad excuses for why they aren't more successful. Denial is like walking through life wearing mental blinders. Even though people operating in denial might verbally communicate a plan of action, they are frequently unaware of the fact that they are unsuccessful in their commitments due to their own lack of responsibility.

Although denial can be an effective defense mechanism, for many people it is a standard of behavior. When it becomes a standard, it's not only dysfunctional; it can be expensive or even dangerous to their health and well-being. People in denial usually don't have a clear perspective on their commitment. They might tell themselves that the commitment is no big deal or that it's something that will take care of itself.

They literally remove it from their conscious thought

and pretend it doesn't exist. It is also common to see traumatized people (those experiencing extreme grief or shock) exhibiting denial. In situations like these, denial serves a temporary and important purpose. It shelters the individual from emotional pain he cannot handle at that time. In the case of trauma, professional help is required to help the individual confront the reality of what has occurred. On a less severe scale, however, denial functions similarly to help people avoid addressing subjects that make them uncomfortable. If a person finds something particularly difficult or unpleasant, he or she might pretend it isn't there or minimize its importance. Again, denial shelters the individual, sometimes in cases where it should not, so the individual is unable to develop and grow.

Martha was an employee sent to me by a company's Employee Assistance Program. Martha was excessively absent from work. In the initial session, I asked Martha to clarify for me what her attendance record was like. (Frequently, there is a pattern to absences that can indicate problems like substance abuse or domestic violence.)

Martha responded that she really wasn't sure how many times she had missed work or exactly when, but that her boss was overreacting. She was absent from work only rarely, she claimed. The number she named was less than half of the actual work days missed. Through further exploration, Martha was able to recognize that because she was angry and resentful that she had been passed over for a promotion, she had lost interest in her current assignment. Her denial regarding her unacceptable attendance record allowed her to avoid confronting her feelings of failure and low self-esteem.

Denial is also frequently observed in smokers who minimize or ignore the health risks of cigarette smoking to avoid the difficulty of battling nicotine addiction. Unfortunately, it is often not until a serious illness is diagnosed that this denial is addressed. These times of crisis are called *teachable moments.* In Martha's case the teachable moment occurred when she faced potential disciplinary action. Had her supervisor not wisely intervened with an EAP referral, her denial would have not only continued to cost the company in lost productivity, but it would probably have cost Martha her job.

Another way denial is manifested is the comparison mentality: I'm not as bad as . . . This line of thinking involves comparing oneself to someone who is worse off, to avoid taking responsibility for making needed changes. For example, a person who needs to lose 30 pounds might justify not taking steps to do so by observing all the people heavier than himself or herself. Although we all compare ourselves to others at times, as part of natural ongoing self-assessment, this form of denial makes unhealthy use of that process. It provides an excuse for inaction. The way to discriminate between a healthy comparison and denial is knowing that lack of action follows denial. There is a significant difference between comparing myself to someone to see how I'm doing, and using the comparison as a justification for doing nothing.

In essence, denial is about avoidance. It serves the purpose of avoiding painful emotions, avoiding difficult tasks, and avoiding self-responsibility.

DISCOURAGEMENT

The discouraged style of thinking is characterized by a negative outlook. Discouraged thinkers view the world through a mental filter that reduces the favorable information and magnifies the negative. They tend to operate from a helpless and hopeless orientation, quick to identify potential (or imagined) obstacles and focus on them. People who are prone to discouragement are also hard to work with, since they typically display low energy and morale.

Another trait of this style is a propensity to see setbacks as failures. Discouraged thinkers will go through a day in which they might do 99 things perfectly right and make one mistake, but they will experience a sense of failure because of the single mistake. They have difficulty incorporating setbacks into the learning process and interpret the setback as further evidence of their incompetence and their doomed future. Because they find fault with themselves in many areas of their lives, they set themselves up for being unable to succeed at keeping commitments.

In the comparison mode, they react in a manner opposite that of denial. Instead of thinking, I'm not as bad as . . . , in the way people in denial would think, discouraged people think, I could never be like . . . They see everyone as so much better off that they could never measure up—depleting personal motivation and preventing them from taking full responsibility. After all, if you can never be like. . . , what's the point of trying?

My interactions with discouraged thinkers, whether in counseling or workplace situations, have often been frustrating. Repeated attempts to suggest positive action or a more upbeat perspective are resisted. People whose thinking tends toward discouragement usually have low self-esteem, and part of their resistance might come from a belief that, If I don't do anything else, I won't fail anymore.

Being discouraged also causes people to continue dysfunctional behaviors, such as smoking or overeating, out of a belief that it's no use to change. This starts a cycle of discouraged thinking, more failure, more discouraged thinking, etc.

OPPOSITIONAL THINKING

Oppositional thinkers have a very strong need for control. They have difficulty with authority and resist direction from others. They expend a great deal of energy defending themselves against being told what to do. Oppositional thinkers prefer to originate ideas; they automatically present alternate approaches to what is suggested to them in an attempt to defy control by others. They also observe the world with the attitude, If I can't do it my way, I won't do it at all. These individuals are hard to influence because of their rigid thinking and immovable attitude.

Ben was one of the most difficult oppositional thinkers I've ever worked with. He was president of a small printing and publishing business. I met with him at the request of the company's board of directors who were concerned about heavy turnover and numerous complaints about his rejection of any feedback about his behavior. Ben was reluctant to schedule the meeting and acted distracted and annoyed during our first encounter.

Besides his hostility and defensiveness, Ben was focused on his assessment of the problem and his idea of a solution. He believed that most people in the company were incapable of making good decisions and needed constant direction. He also believed that in a conflictual situation, the way to really get things done was to push harder. Obviously, Ben possessed determination and a strong will. However, in times of stress when the heat was on, he overused his strengths and alienated others. This was a real challenge for me as a consultant since any advice offered to an oppositional thinker tends to be met with strong opposition.

In order to be effective with Ben, I had to position myself as an ally and not another force working against him. I began by empathizing with the pressure he was under and expressed the thought that it must be frustrating and overwhelming to be in his position. After an hour or two of neutral discussion concerning the problems he faced with turnover, Ben was more receptive to my views and perceptions. We were able to collaborate on a plan for retaining employees and improving company morale.

EXTERNALIZED THINKING

Externalized thinkers sometimes come across as victims. They believe their failure (and sometimes their success) is due primarily to forces outside themselves. Their moods are more strongly influenced by changing events than those of the average person. This hypersensitivity to outside forces is a result of a mental outlook quite different from that of the oppositional thinker. The person with externalized thinking waits for the world to turn one way or another and decide his fate. Externalized thinkers observe situations around them and think, If things were different, I wouldn't feel this way. This style of thinking is reactive rather than responsive—as though the person is a pinball in the great pinball machine of life. This way of thinking can also result in a critical or judgmental attitude.

Keep in mind that all of us exhibit these disruptive styles to some degree. We have all experienced some form of discouragement and tend to deny what is threatening or painful to us. Difficulty with issues of control can cause us to become oppositional at times or to hold others responsible for our lives. The point is that when these styles of thinking become a dominant pattern in our lives, they can be disruptive to commitments.

It is also possible for an individual to display a combination of these styles and exhibit them differently and to varying degrees, depending on the situation. When this is the case, the strategies offered later in the chapter will still apply. It's just that it might be necessary to use many different strategies for certain individuals.

THE VOICE OF COMMITMENT

What we say about our company, the people with whom we work, and the customers to whom we relate are reflections of our thinking process. Listening to one's words can provide important insights when it comes to commitments. It doesn't take a highly trained professional ear to hear what people think about their commitments. Some suggestions offered in this section will help managers assess the commitments of their workers by listening to key phrases and themes in communication.

DENIERS: WHAT TO LISTEN FOR

What we hear most from people in denial is either an outright challenge to the issue, a reluctance to discuss it, or a pretense that it doesn't matter. Denial can also take the form of humor to distract you and get you off the subject.

There are three trends to look for in our own thinking and in the words of others: *rationalization, inappropriate use of humor,* and *open denial.* Let's take a closer look at each.

RATIONALIZATION

We use rationalization to justify and feel more comfortable with imperfections. Obviously, rationalization has a positive function. We don't live in a perfect world. However, when rationalization is used to allow for dysfunctional behavior or protect someone else unnecessarily, it can interfere with commitment. It is helpful to listen for rationalizations, especially when we are attacked or criticized. A comment like, Your work is unacceptable, can be followed with our own rationalization of, My work would be fine if I had a good boss.

INAPPROPRIATE USE OF HUMOR

A popular way of dealing with discomfort is to attempt to laugh it away. Although there is a place for humor, especially in our stressful and overly serious lives, this form of humor can be problematic. There are times when we continually avoid issues through the use of humor, and as a result, we never address the reality of the situation. This is a difficult type of denial to assess because we might be attempting to reassure or comfort others by being funny. One way to minimize the importance of a commitment is to use humor in a deprecating manner, such as with biting sarcasm.

OPEN DENIAL

This is the most obvious form of denial. In a way, it's the easiest to identify and change. With open denial, we aren't totally denying the situation, we're merely presenting a strong noncommittal view. This is different from op-

positional thinking because we're not presenting an oppositional view; we're merely claiming that it's not an issue.
Statements in this category are ones like, If we just ignore
it, it'll take care of itself, and, Look at my father, he
smoked every day of his life and he lived to be 90.

DISCOURAGED THINKERS: WHAT TO LISTEN FOR

The voice of discouragement can be expressed in three
areas: self-discouragement, situational discouragement,
and a discouraged view of the future.

Self-discouragement is manifested in statements concerning a person's inadequacy and lack of confidence,
such as, I'm just not any good at this, or, I don't have what
it takes to succeed at this. It is a reflection of a negative
self-image and shows up as self-criticism and self-blame.
Frequent references to past failures are heard, along with
pronouncements of personal flaws and weaknesses.

Situational discouragement is reflected in negative
statements about circumstances and events, such as, You
can't trust anybody, and, We've tried this before and it
didn't work.

When this negative view is aimed at the future and
clouds expectations, it reflects the third form, discouraged
view of the future. A person who thinks this way says,
Things are only going to get worse, or, I'm never going to
get promoted. Even if these statements can be facts, the
key is to listen for a pattern. This will help reveal the
strength of an individual's commitment.

The discouraged view of the future is different from
self-discouragement because self-discouragement is centered on faults from within. The person discouraged

about the future is in a different victim mode, feeling that the world is a negative place and therefore won't deliver what he or she wants.

▌ OPPOSITIONAL THINKERS: WHAT TO LISTEN FOR

The voice of opposition can be loud and forceful or subtle and insidious. It's fairly easy to identify oppositional statements when they are verbalized. They often take the form of adamant or arbitrary disagreement and/or disapproval. More subtle manifestations of this type of thinking take the form of sniping or gossip.

Once, while I was working out at the company fitness center, an employee in my department passed by and made a comment in front of other executives, who were also working out nearby. He said, "Boy, I can't wait to be at your level and get paid to work out on company time!" The ingratiating smile on his face and his genial tone belied his intended message, which when translated was, You get paid more and work less than us underlings. Later I became aware of other comments this individual made out of my earshot. This confirmed my view that he was not committed to our team goals but rather to his own agenda.

▌ EXTERNALIZED THINKERS: WHAT TO LISTEN FOR

Externalized thinkers blame and criticize in an other-focused manner. Frequent use of words like they, them, him, and her (as opposed to "I") reflect this style of thinking. Chronic blaming or criticism emanates from the externalized thinker in statements such as, If only they would, Why are they making us, and, It's not fair!

Denial, discouragement, and warped thinking via opposition and externalization erode commitment on two levels. They not only infect an individual's commitment; they can infect others who are more committed. Managers who can properly identify these unhelpful forms of thought can try to redirect the individual's style and renew a sense of commitment.

▎THE ACTIONS OF COMMITMENT

The most telling evidence of true integration lies in a person's actions. Often called "walking your talk," regularly engaging in behaviors that support commitment is the final necessary condition for success. When disruptive styles of thinking come into play, an individual is unable to consistently sustain the behaviors required for commitment. There are distinct similarities in the behavioral responses to each of the disruptive cognitive styles earlier discussed. All result in a lack of follow-through and an absence of positive action.

Oppositional thinking manifests itself more actively than the other three, taking the form of a more visible set of negative behaviors. Much like taking a reluctant dog on a walk, the harder the leash is pulled in one direction, the more the dog tugs at it in the other. Working with a person who thinks oppositionally can feel like a pointless struggle. This is especially true when the manager's style tends toward the dominant, or if the manager tries to use pressure or force.

Somewhat less obvious, but equally frustrating, is noncompliance. An employee operating in this manner might actually refuse to do what he or she is asked or might mildly verbalize agreement but deliberately not follow through.

Noncompliance is also a characteristic of denial. Physicians often express the futility of working with patients who discontinue medication against doctor's orders or eat a high-fat diet after being warned of high cholesterol levels. These patients deny the seriousness of their illness and abandon responsible behaviors. Another form of denial is procrastination. I have frequently observed people in downsizing organizations who postpone updating their resumes and networking. They avoid confronting the issue because of the immense fear of losing their jobs.

Discouraged and externalized thinking are often manifested passively, too. Inactivity characterized by lethargy and a low energy level is typical of discouraged thinking. Self-sabotaging or self-destructive behavior, such as neglecting important projects or absenteeism, might also suggest this mode of thinking. Like denial, externalized thinking often shows up as procrastination, as the individual waits for someone else to make things happen. This heavy reliance on others often prevents the person from taking positive action. In the workplace, it's easy to see how this can slow the progress of work efforts and undermine productivity. On a personal level, externalized thinking can prevent people from achieving their goals. It damages feelings of accomplishment and empowerment.

It is important for managers to know that any of these dysfunctional behaviors can suggest more serious and problematic conditions. If discouraged thinking shows up as a comprehensive inability to function, or oppositional thinking takes the form of overt hostility, the individual might require professional assistance. In severe cases such as these, the manager should not try to tackle the problem, but rather, call on the assistance of a psychologist.

STRATEGIES FOR DEALING WITH DISRUPTIVE COGNITIVE STYLES

Once these disruptive strategies are recognized, the challenge for managers is to assist employees in correcting them. Different styles of thinking require different defensive techniques, interaction, and direction.

DENIAL

The biggest challenge in working with denial is to hold the person accountable. Once a goal or plan of action is stated, the person will need to be monitored or supported. It is important not to get caught up in the person's rationalizations for their lack of follow-through. Stay focused on goals and performance; present the individual's behavior to him as evidence. Provide ongoing reminders of the importance of the commitment.

DISCOURAGEMENT

Stressing the positive is essential with discouraged thinkers. However, it is imperative that positive statements come from the individual as well as the manager. Pep talks are unlikely to be successful unless they are linked to the individual's demonstrated behaviors and the manager is able to convince the employee that the success is larger than setbacks.

Create opportunities for daily success to battle the big picture negative that discouraged thinkers employ. Push them to verbalize their own success; this will help them to see themselves in a more positive light. Also, be aware of how easy it is for others to absorb negativity. This can quickly drain energy from a team. Watching carefully for this kind of contagious discouragement will help keep it from affecting teamwork.

OPPOSITIONAL THINKING

Whenever possible, allow oppositional thinkers to provide input. Try to solicit their ideas before asking them to execute a project. They need to feel included in the process and instrumental to the plan.

Be flexible regarding how they perform tasks. They might need more brainstorming than you'd prefer, but it will be time well spent on your part if it prevents having to put out fires later.

Since oppositional thinking is also a way to express frustrations and anger unrelated to the issue at hand, inquire about the emotion that is being expressed. This can be done in the form of a question, such as, You seem to be expressing a lot of anger. Does it all come from this project, or are there other things going on that are making you angry?

If the struggle with an oppositional thinker continues after your best efforts, it might be necessary to simply let go. A manager can abandon efforts to persuade, and remove the individual from a particular project. In a case of noncompliance, it might be necessary to document the resistance and take appropriate disciplinary action. The point at which to make such a decision will depend on a manager's judgment and the nature of the situation. Keep in mind that for many oppositional thinkers, the struggle itself is gratifying and meets deeply set personal needs. Engaging in power plays often provides an outlet for the oppositional thinker's personal psychological agenda and goes beyond the scope of work issues. A manager in this situation will want to preserve his or her own energy rather than fight a losing battle; continuing to engage in the struggle will only reinforce oppositional behavior.

EXTERNALIZED THINKING

Be specific about your expectations regarding the performance of externalized thinkers. You might have to continually remind them of their particular role in any effort to counteract their tendency to avoid responsibility. One method of facilitating this is coaching the employee to use *I* statements unless he is clearly representing a group.

In a meeting I attended, Debbie, one of several managers, made the statement, "Branch managers don't feel included in the decision-making process." Actually, other branch managers were quite comfortable with the decision-making process of senior management. Another manager voiced his opposition to Debbie's statement and asked her to restate her perspective as hers, not the group's. By owning the thought and feeling concerning the decision-making process, Debbie communicated her thoughts more accurately.

Externalizers are quick to point out how "we" are feeling, or what "we" don't like, or whether "we" have ever discussed it as a group or not! They need to be consistently reminded to own their own opinions and present them as personal, not group perceptions.

Point out what the person has done successfully independent of the actions of others. To build self-efficacy with externalized thinkers, it's important to have them stay centered on their own unique skills and talents—linking a particular skill to a proven outcome.

▌ The Mindset of Commitment

Integration is not an easy step to achieve, particularly for people who lack self-awareness and have difficulty recognizing the pitfalls that they create for themselves. However, it does not have to be inordinately time consuming for a manager to lead individuals to productive and satisfying integration.

Pointing out when people are consistent in their commitments, through periodic feedback and recognition, and through confrontation when there are inconsistencies, will help people stay focused. This will also create the understanding that commitments are not only verbal statements of intent, but are observable behaviors as well.

Truly committed people don't spend much time consciously thinking about their commitments. The commitments are part of the fabric of their lives. When our commitments become fully integrated, we no longer have to work as hard at keeping them at the fore. They become almost automatic, like remembering to lock the door when we leave the house.

Questions to Facilitate Consistency and Integration

1. Are you thinking, saying, and doing those things that exemplify your commitment?

2. Do you frequently talk yourself out of doing those things that prove your commitment?

3. What can you change *today* that will help you to be more integrated with your commitment?

Key Points in This Chapter

- A true commitment is maintained consistently and with passion.

- Four disruptive styles can prevent successful completion of commitments. These are denial, discouragement, oppositional thinking, and externalized thinking.

- Managers can successfully deal with these disruptive styles by using appropriate information and actions.

7

ORGANIZATIONAL COMMITMENT:

Creating a Culture of Support and Motivation

Imagine that you have interviewed for a job at an innovative company, where you will be instrumental in developing an information network. It will allow people to share technologic breakthroughs instantly on an interactive computer system. You are clear on how the system will operate, and you've done research on similar programs that have succeeded and failed.

In addition, you have accepted the potential gains and sacrifices you will make to carry out this project and have even explored the emotional and mental barriers that might affect your performance. You have taken steps to make this program a reality and you are confident of your abilities. You anticipate a favorable outcome. You have successfully progressed through the factors of commitment and are poised for the challenge.

You are hired for the job. Then you find that the boss requires all decisions, even minor ones, to go through him. Financial resources are allocated to existing projects rather than new ideas. Your peers greet the concept with remarks like, But we've never done it that way—why start now?

Unfortunately, thousands of individuals have had this

type of experience at any given time. A high level of commitment by an employee is watered down, pushed down, or even beaten down by a nonsupportive corporate culture. Unfortunately, this type of situation is not limited to bright people starting new jobs. Employees who have spent years working for the same company can find themselves in a similar situation. An essential component for personal commitments to thrive is a corporate culture that supports and encourages them.

Organizational culture is the total complex of ideas, values, and common behaviors that a group of people share. At times these components are highly visible and easily recognized—like a dress code. Mission statements are another form, existing in print and expressed through corporate values and ethics. Culture also possesses more subtle elements, however, that influence in powerful ways. These influences are unwritten rules and standards of behavior (often called norms) that people adopt and comply with as a condition of belonging to the group.

Much like an old family recipe, culture is a human creation inherited and passed on to the next generation of users. As each new group assumes ownership, they might modify and enhance it to suit current needs or conditions. Traditionally, corporate culture has been slow to change and has been predictable. But the last few years have changed that. With the coming of the information age, worldwide economic influences, and accelerated lifestyle change, many ingredients in the recipe have been replaced or modified. Not only have the ingredients been changed; the methods of preparation have been altered, too. Companies have made the transition from a bowl and wooden spoon to the food processor and microwave in a brief time.

It is rare today to attend a meeting that is not interrupted by beeping pagers and cellular phones. It is no longer rare to have a teleconferenced meeting with people around the world. Information once communicated person to person is now transmitted between pieces of hardware. It recalls what is fast becoming an old joke: I'll have my answering machine call your answering machine.

With the mind-boggling rate and degree of change we are experiencing, it's more important than ever to identify the core ingredients of human behavior that are key to present-day success and worthy of being passed to future generations. These will have a powerful impact on how commitment is shaped and maintained.

DYNAMICS OF A CULTURE OF COMMITMENT

1. CREATE A CLEAR VISION AND COMMUNICATE IT COMPREHENSIVELY

In Chapter 3, I outlined the importance of vision in creating the intent and strength of any commitment and the concomitant organizational responsibilities. In Chapter 4, I also outlined core motivational criteria that establish an environment suitable for high performance. A closer examination of these issues is essential for a complete understanding of their roles in organizational culture.

Providing ongoing communication of information related to the organization's mission statements, goals, and objectives makes it possible for individuals and groups to effectively measure progress toward the goal. It also sends an important message that people are valued enough to be kept informed and up to date. This creates a norm of shared responsibility in which knowledge vital to success is accessible to those who need it; it doesn't become the property of a privileged few. This inclusive approach creates shared vision, which is essential for sustained commitment. Being clear about the direction of the company will prevent uncertainty and confusion, which are the result of conflicting views and ambiguity. An organization that lacks shared vision fosters mistrust and low productivity. And the most predictable human response to being excluded is to become self-protective and territorial. In the old exclusive type of culture, political machinations thrived and subgroups jockeyed for power and control. Today's successful business can no longer afford this waste of creative energy and diffused loyalty.

A hospital I worked with several years ago illustrates this phenomenon. Conflicts between four primary divisions of the hospital, lasting several years, contributed to poor morale, loss of market share, and a dysfunctional work environment. In the initial meeting, I discovered that none of the department heads could articulate the hospital's mission statement. When someone finally unearthed a copy of it, it was so obscure and vaguely worded that even the president wasn't clear what it meant!

The situation had reached a point of crisis. There were overlaps in objectives, causing duplication of services and internal competition—and wasting of valuable resources. A climate of territoriality stifled communication between groups and eroded relationships that had been mutually supportive and productive. Patients were confused and frustrated when they attempted to obtain needed services. The corporate culture was secretive, dishonest, closed, and indirect.

By contrast, organizations that function inclusively

have a global vision that most people can personally relate to. The vision is actively shared among groups. This results in a better understanding of how work fits into the total plan. It helps clarify roles and responsibilities, minimizing duplication of effort. With information flowing freely and amicably, people are more likely to operate from a base of trust and be engaged and motivated.

Long-term visions can be kept alive with short-term news of success. As stated earlier, some organizations establish a vision that requires long-term productivity, and then offer no intermittent rest stops on the way to achieving that vision. Without ongoing support, it's tough to create long-term viability in vision.

2. PROVIDE STELLAR LEADERSHIP

The ultimate goal of any leader—whether the coach of an athletic team or president of a Fortune 500 company—is to inspire and elicit superior performance from all individuals in the organization. The style by which this high performance is generated has changed through the ages and continues to evolve. The coaching tactics of Vince Lombardi and Woody Hayes (forceful, intimidating, and threatening) were highly effective in the 50s, 60s, and 70s, when followers were more complacent and obedient. However, that style is quite different from the coaching style of Pat Riley and Bill Parcells, with 1990s-style success. A more participative, problem-solving, and less abrasive approach is needed.

The same trend occurred in the business setting. Leadership through intimidation and fear might have worked in an environment that offered job security in exchange for compliance. However, since job security is no longer the guarantee, people have changed—and new strategies are required. Threats of getting fired no longer hold the same power. Some people still fear losing their jobs, but the reality of downsizing and outsourcing has caused more people to assume their jobs are ephemeral anyway. Work ethics have also matured so that people expect to be treated with dignity and respect. The result is a more sophisticated workforce that demands esteem.

The effective leader of the 90s must be a living example of what it takes for his or her particular team to succeed. All the components of commitment must be ensconced in the heart, mind, and soul of the leader and demonstrated regularly. The commitment must be lived. A highly visible leader who exemplifies corporate values by his actions will influence culture more rapidly and effectively than a low-profile leader or one who displays inconsistent behaviors. More than ever, people are watching and observing people who walk the talk. This high level of integrity is a necessary requirement for success in today's work environment. Coupled with this is the fact that leaders must be very careful about what they promise, because delivering on promises is what most people look for as a sign of true commitment. Shooting from the hip or saying things merely to placate employees are poor ways to demonstrate leadership.

With a clear point of convergence outlined for everyone to follow, the leader sets the target and determines priorities. What leaders pay attention to and measure will ultimately result in a display of corresponding behaviors. Merely stating a corporate direction or priority will get people's attention, but measuring the stated behaviors will lead to embedding them into the culture. Savvy managers know this well and are in tune with the formal and informal messages of key leaders. In addition to formal statements of corporate philosophy and creed, casual remarks and inquiries that are consistently focused on a particular area can send strong messages of importance and precedence. Communication by the leadership of an organization also helps commitments when it:

- Attempts to understand the needs and ideas of people and incorporates these ideas into observable actions.

- Allows for people to disagree without negative consequences.

- Is open, honest, and direct.

Various ways of communicating throughout an organization were covered in Chapter 3, and a fuller exploration of potential in this area would be a publication in itself. The objective for leadership communication is to create an environment of reciprocal respect, involvement, and consistent focus on the defined values and goals of the organization.

The role of every manager in an organization also includes leadership responsibilities. The responsibilities outlined above must also be incorporated in the ongoing functions of managers. Although the scope of influence of the manager might not be as great as that of the leader of an organization, the impact on specific individuals might actually be more powerful because of the day-to-day contact.

Much like the coach of a sports team, the manager spends a lot of time instructing, encouraging, and motivating individuals to their best performance. Various styles of management go beyond the scope of this book and most managers already have an assortment of strategies to use. However, it's important to consider styles of management that reinforce or interfere with commitments.

To begin with, it's helpful to consider the person first and then determine the appropriate style to use. I once used this approach very effectively when working with a college basketball team whose coach asked me to help with tension that some players were experiencing during the games. At first I thought I was being asked to teach basic stress management and relaxation skills to the players and instruct them on how to channel stress in productive ways. In a short time I realized that the coach was having trouble with players on the team, especially their key player who had been recruited from a high-ranking regional rival. In working with the team I used an assessment instrument along with the Profile of Mood States, which provides information on particular triggers to certain moods. This information was used with the coach to determine the best coaching style to use with the players.

In the case of their recruited superstar, it was determined that he responded best to noninstructional strategies, such as encouragement and off-line talks about areas of improvement. This player also shared with me that he was extremely embarrassed when the coach instructed him in front of other members of the team, such as teaching him how to perform a certain move or execute a particular play. This embarrassment resulted in severe oppositional behavior. He was not resistant to suggestions for improvement but when these instructions were *demonstrated*, he reacted. Other players on the team were quite different. In fact, some players *wanted* and welcomed the coach's demonstrations and felt they were helpful.

By flexing his methods with individual players, the coach created an environment where team members felt attended to and were not all treated in the same manner. This not only reduced tension but also made it possible for individuals to develop much more rapidly and with considerably more fun.

In addition to the previously mentioned aspects of communication, the manager must also attend to providing feedback on an ongoing basis and facilitating cross-functional communication. The best intention of key leaders to open communication between functions can be stifled unless managers actively engage in and support this through cross-function networking and collaboration. One of the most powerful determinants of success in business as we move into the next century will be the effectiveness of cross-functional teams to identify problems and collaborate in solving them. This is crucial to commitments because it broadens the base of support and facilitates integration of thoughts and ideas with team behavior.

Cross-functional partnership can also minimize conflict that occurs in territorial organizations. Experienced managers know that conflict can serve a constructive purpose by identifying important issues that need to be resolved. However, the destructive conflict that results from divisional competition becomes an outmoded way of operating when teams collaborate on their mutual commitment to collective goals.

3. PROVIDE REWARDS, RECOGNITION, AND COMPENSATION

Any stated objective or organizational goal without reinforcement or incentive is unlikely to become a reality.

Like a car with no gasoline, no matter how great it looks, it's not going anywhere. A basic tenet of human nature is to initiate and sustain behavior either to achieve a positive result or to avoid a negative one. As stated earlier, the threat of job loss or disciplinary action is losing its effectiveness as a motivational tool. Offering people rewards and acknowledgment for their efforts is more in line with individual needs for accomplishment and involvement. (This defines the new view of career and success.) It is essential that incentives are tied in measurable and observable ways to corporate values.

One company I worked with had issued employee satisfaction surveys for several years. They expressed a desire to create an environment of trust and engagement. However, few of the managers acted on the results of the surveys. Progress was slow and sporadic, and though issuing the surveys gave the impression that the company cared and wanted to keep employees happy, it was all smoke and mirrors, with little action.

Then the company decided to make management compensation contingent in part upon the survey results. With a financial incentive to change behavior, many sluggish managers quickly took action on the survey results and worked to create more involvement.

A colleague of mine dealt with a situation that clearly outlines how a company can falter at enforcing its stated values. This colleague was called on to analyze a department in a company noted for its new family-friendly work environment. Child care subsidies, parental leave, and flexible work arrangements, including telecommuting, were some family-friendly options offered the employees. But this department, headed by a manager we'll call Sharon, showed a deep drop in productivity and morale.

"The telecommuting policy is the problem," Sharon stated to my colleague, who served as an organizational consultant. Sharon said she was opposed to the policy at the outset and believed her employees were in need of closer supervision than was possible when they worked from home one or two days a week. She suspected her staff used telecommuting days for personal activities and even referred to them as days off.

Other departments, even those that had a high number of telecommuters, showed significant improvement with the new policies. So what was the problem?

Focus groups revealed that Sharon was the problem. Although she couldn't deny her staff the opportunity to work a few days at home, she expressed her dislike of the policy. Employees cited examples of how Sharon would "forget" to mention (to an employee working at home that day) an important meeting or a conference call. The same employees would be held responsible for information discussed in their absence. Sharon would respond, "Oh, I guess you were *off* that day." She would also call employees working from home several times a day to "check in." To the employees this translated as being checked up on. Requests to telecommute were agreed to and scheduled with much impatience and reluctance on Sharon's part.

In a summary meeting, the president of the company explained to Sharon that other departments were using telecommuting to their advantage. He also expressed to her that as a manager, she had the responsibility to support company policy, not just comply with it. Sharon recognized that her high need for control and lack of empathy for family values had interfered with her commitment to uphold the values of the organization. She began to modify her interactions with the people she managed and the department began to experience improvement in morale and productivity.

A potentially powerful source of motivation for employees continues to be performance appraisals. Unfortunately, this institutionalized feedback and evaluation tool is often underutilized or used ineffectively. Because yearly appraisal sessions can be emotionally loaded, especially in the case of unsatisfactory performance, they are frequently postponed and so brief in nature that they provide little constructive information. Also, since in today's flatter organizations managers have many more fish to fry, appraisals become just another project in the in-box heap.

If managers expect commitment from employees, though, they must recognize the immense value of the appraisal process. The most effective performance appraisal is one that includes recognition for efforts made along with feedback on the employee's commitment, using the four cornerstones of commitment mentioned in this book.

Managers who are afraid to guide employees' work by correctly using appraisals might be tempted to give everyone a great review. This backfires because (1) employees don't see it as real praise, and (2) they must consistently be given great reviews or it may appear as though they've begun to do poorly.

A devastating review, however, can backfire in other ways. I knew of a situation in which a man received such a critical performance review that he was soon on disability for an emotional disorder.

Bolstering commitment doesn't begin and end with the performance appraisal. It is important to reinforce individual commitments by praising often and whenever possible, especially in the presence of others. Immediate recognition for a job well done or for demonstrated teamwork is the fuel we all need to perform at our best.

4. CULTIVATE INDIVIDUAL DEVELOPMENT

One of the most effective ways of assuring individual commitments to organizational goals is to align abilities of employees to appropriate jobs or modify (design) jobs to capitalize on the strengths of individuals. People are more likely to follow through on their personal commitments when they are involved in activities that are meaningful and enjoyable. A wide range of tools are available to managers to assess unique talents, preferences, and work styles of employees. Instruments such as the Myers-Briggs Type Indicator, Performax, and Strong-Campbell Interest Inventory have been used to enhance communication, build teams, and delegate work according to the characteristics of the person.

Another instrument I have personally used to assess individual and team dynamics is the Insight Inventory, developed by Dr. Patrick Handley of the Insight Institute, Kansas City, Missouri. This profiling system provides valuable information in the form of preferred styles of relating to people, handling details, eliciting support, and dealing with the pace of activity. In addition to work preferences, the individual learns about preferences in personal life that might be quite different from how they function on the job. This information is helpful in determining tasks in which the individual will likely succeed, areas for improving communication, potentially stressful activities, and opportunities for capitalizing on team performance. I have seen managers use this information very effectively and have been part of team efforts where managers utilized it to modify existing tasks so that team members could support and contribute to each other's success. Instruments of this sort can be powerful enhancers for building commitment because they match the employee's innate abilities to the performance of the task at hand. They might also improve the individual's perceived ability to control his work by incorporating specific skills.

5. EMPOWER

Empowerment is a process whereby employees understand the rationale of the business, share decision making, and experience accountability. It is hard to find a company in the U.S. today that doesn't have some sort of empowerment initiative. The reason, beyond the obvious efficiencies in the work process, is that through involvement and ownership comes commitment.

When properly implemented, empowerment can be a key factor in the new employee contract that states, I can't guarantee lifetime employment, but I can offer you opportunities to learn and develop and engage you in the work process. It sounds great and makes perfect sense. So why do so many empowerment efforts struggle? Part of the reason is the turbulence of change, as discussed in Chapter 5. For some people there is hesitation in giving up long-held control and decision-making authority that goes along with traditional management roles. This can also be threatening if there is a perception of reduced importance and diminished worth.

It is easy to imagine how it would feel to a manager who for 20 years made all the important decisions in a department and now must allow others to make decisions independently. Not only is 20 years of authority and control at risk, but also the self-esteem that goes along with territorial ownership. On the flip side, there might be an employee who already feels overwhelmed by a demanding workload. If that employee is asked to take on decision-making responsibilities as well, he or she might feel imposed upon rather than empowered.

A viable implementation strategy for incorporating the spirit and work benefits of empowerment is *personalization of the process*. Literally, this means that employees have input into whether or not they make decisions and they are allowed to progress through decision making based on their experience and level of comfort. It's unreasonable to assume that everyone is capable of making all of the many decisions that must be made on a daily basis. It's also unlikely that every manager is willing to waive decisions that have important potential outcomes. What is possible is to have managers allocate responsibility according to ability and inclination. In order for this collaboration to work, two things are required: (1) training must be offered to develop skills and abilities, and (2) people must be allowed to experience setbacks and learn from these experiences without unnecessary ridicule and reprimand.

As a final point in the exploration of organizational culture, I strongly advocate the use of instruments and processes which have the capability to define culture in a specific and tangible way. These tools (usually referred to as culture audits) utilize a carefully constructed survey format to solicit employee feedback on crucial issues related to aspects of the organizational culture. Data gleaned from the audits can provide significant insights into needed changes in such areas as training, facilitation of performance, interaction between managers and subordinates, emotional involvement (on the part of employees) in the job, and supportiveness of the climate, as well as more specifically business-focused issues like customer relations and quality. One such instrument, developed by Dr. Rick Bellingham of Possibilities, Inc., Basking Ridge, New Jersey, provides a comprehensive assessment of corporate culture on 11 dimensions:

Goal setting

Communications

Customer satisfaction

Process management (how the work gets done)

Leadership

Clarity of vision

Teamwork

Decision making

Individual development

Trust

Quality

A culture audit not only serves the purpose of assessing and profiling a company's work environment to determine areas of strength or deficiencies, but it can be used as a post-test for determining the success of various initiatives.

Dr. Bellingham's instrument measures the areas mentioned above in the context of descriptive norms that define each component of culture. Respondents rate each norm in a given area in terms of its strength (how true is this of our culture?), its importance (how significant is the norm to me?) and its direction (is it getting worse, better, or staying the same?). Finally, the ten most important norms are identified and evaluated with regard to gaps between strength and importance. This helps to determine problem areas within the culture.

It is important to recognize that a culture audit is more than just another survey. We have all had the experience of completing surveys thoughtfully and devoting time and energy to them, only to find out later that the resulting information ended up in someone's filing cabinet, unused. When this occurs, surveys only serve to generate frustration (due to the reasonable assumption by respondents that the data were being compiled for some positive purpose). Leaders who are truly committed to making positive changes in organizational culture must do more than solicit feedback. Defining the culture in its present context is only the first step. An effective culture audit will not only address issues that go deeper than symptoms and actually explore underlying causes; it will also provide a springboard for the process of change to begin. By defining an ideal culture, and comparing it to the present one, leaders can proceed to create plans for making and sustaining needed changes at a level that will have real impact on commitment.

Since the days of Sigmund Freud, psychologists have maintained that significant patterns of behavior arise out of the unconscious mind of the individual. It has been observed countless times that people behave in ways that don't work well for them any longer or are even destructive because of a set of unwritten rules or agendas. These rules and agendas are based on past experience and ways of relating that are not consciously expressed but are very firmly ingrained. The same can be said for organizations, and this concept is crucial to the understanding of culture change. Often a new set of procedures or an effort to change management styles is introduced, only to be diluted or sabotaged by a powerful organizational unconscious, which dictates that people behave otherwise.

Attempts to explore and modify the cultures of organizations must address this deeper level of beliefs and surface the true underlying normative expectations that govern patterns of behavior. Culture audits are an effective method of surfacing the "unconscious mind" of an organization. Once the unwritten rules are written and thus made tangible, efforts to implement change are more likely to be successful.

Key Points in This Chapter

- Because the workplace has been reshaped by societal change, a new type of commitment must be generated.

- Victimization is a current trend in which employees feel that work satisfaction and stability are out of their control.

- Managers can create a new, superior type of loyalty by meeting the needs of today's worker.

- Decisiveness, ambition, obligation, and guarantees are not commitment. Commitment comprises a set of reliable behaviors that create success.

8

BUILDING COMMITMENT WITH TEAMS
Why Teams Are Important

When I think about teams in the context of a supportive culture, I remember the neighborhood I was raised in. My neighborhood was comprised mainly of Italian immigrants, most of whom had large families and little money. The predominant value within the community was to provide the best life possible for families given the limited resources. I don't remember anyone who had a professional career. Most families maintained traditional roles with the father as breadwinner (usually a manual laborer) and the mother as homemaker.

Something all families had in common was genuine caring for each other that went beyond the nuclear family to include the entire community. Everyone contributed through their unique talents or interests.

Many people made homemade wine, and one neighbor, Giuseppe, was a master at this. He shared his expertise and equipment with others, who tried to match the richness and quality of his product. Pasquale had bounteous peach and pear trees and I can still see his weathered, smiling face as he offered a portion of his annual harvest to my mother for canning and preserving. Nunzio's house was where all the kids in the neighborhood went to get their hair cut—not because he was a barber, but because he had the tools and skill for keeping us neat and groomed. For this service he was lavishly paid 50 cents.

My father, Arthur, had a wonderful garden, the envy of the neighborhood. I delivered sacks full of tomatoes, cucumbers, zucchini, and peppers to appreciative families who lived nearby. We even had a man who made bleach in his basement who would barter it for items of food or in exchange for other services. If someone needed transportation outside of the neighborhood, Pete (one of the few people who owned a car) was always willing to provide taxi service. Even though he was so short he could barely see over the steering wheel and his top speed was 20 miles an hour, he could always be relied on to get you where you wanted to go.

Perhaps even more than the men, the women of the community typified a spirit of cohesive support. Moms were virtually interchangeable and I remember the security of knowing I could go to any woman in the neighborhood and be fed something or have a cut bandaged. Child care was truly a cooperative effort, particularly if there were illness in a family, death, or the birth of a new baby. Kids from different families shared each other's dinner tables on a regular basis. Women helped each other with household tasks, provided pots of soup, platters of spaghetti, or a listening ear in times of need. Coffee was always hot on the stove and the door was always open for company who never waited to be invited and always received a warm welcome.

The quality of life in this neighborhood was remarkable considering the economic limitations people faced. It was largely attributable to the cooperative, mutually supportive value system they shared. No single family operating independently could have experienced the level of well-being and comfort that the community created together. Neighborhoods like mine have become something of an anachronism in modern society, but they are a testimony to the power of people working together toward a common goal, and an authentic illustration of a whole that is far greater than the sum of its parts.

Throughout my professional career I have occasionally had the experience of observing this kind of cohesion in action. There is a special chemistry among people who work well together that enables them to accomplish some amazing things. This synergy is in part the result of maximizing individual talents and strengths and channeling them in a shared direction. Respecting and utilizing each person's unique capabilities benefits the team exponentially and provides each member with a sense of purpose and belonging. This experience, in turn, contributes to individual self-esteem, which is a necessary resource for productivity.

High-functioning teams also incorporate diverse perspectives, which can clarify important issues and facilitate the creation of workable ideas. Individuals working and deciding alone have the opinion of one and often fail to recognize or fully understand diverse views. Even the most heartfelt and sincere intentions will fall short of full potential without input from others. The wisdom that occurs because of member contributions can result in decisions that are effective and equitable. Working with the support of a team, people are empowered to take risks and experiment, creatively knowing they can rely on co-workers to aid their efforts.

Simply stated, teams are crucial for success because

they accomplish together what individuals cannot do separately. In today's business setting, a sense of community spirit will be the hallmark of thriving organizations. The sense of identity and belonging that people once derived from a neighborhood, community, or the old company must now be provided by membership in a high-performing team. This will prove to be an essential ingredient in maintaining a loyal and highly committed workforce.

DYNAMICS OF HIGH-PERFORMANCE TEAMS

The foundation of any high-performance team is based on a shared vision and shared accountability. This establishes the base for a group commitment to a common purpose and a willingness of each individual to contribute to that end. Truly successful teams devote energy and time to create, modify, and achieve consensus for a purpose in which not only the group, but each individual, has ownership. Defining vision is an ongoing process rather than a task to be accomplished, because goals and objectives are constantly changing and vision might take on new dimensions as a result. Collective accountability consists of genuine commitments people make to each other and to themselves. This helps the development of trust. Trust is at the core of any team that performs well. In exchange for loyalty to the team's objectives, individuals receive the opportunity to express their views and needs and be listened to with respect. Trust and accountability cannot be forced on people. These factors do, however, tend to be a natural by-product when individuals invest time and energy in defining a common goal and how it is to be accomplished.

My wife and I discovered that an effective means of persuading our seven-year-old son to eat healthy food was to involve him in the planning and preparation of meals. Not only did this create a greater sense of ownership on his part, but the shared activity benefited our relationship with him as well. Seeing himself as a valued participant in a necessary function was good for his self-esteem and occasionally even motivated him to help with the cleanup!

A method that has been effectively used by team leaders is establishment of *team norms* to define and clarify expectations and agreed-upon mutual responsibilities. The process is relatively simple.

Step 1. On a flip chart or blackboard, list the ideal team behaviors, which in the group's collective view represent optimal cooperation and effectiveness. Categorize these behaviors in terms of:

- Communication

- Rewards and recognition

- Support

- Participation

- Shared satisfaction

- Enjoyment

For example, the norms of starting and ending meetings at the scheduled time and everyone offering an opinion would be in the category *Participation*. An open door policy by the team leader would be included in *Communication*.

Step 2. Compare the ideal norms to existing norms of previous teams in which people have participated. For instance, the prevailing norm might be that scheduled meetings typically begin 15 to 20 minutes late and extend beyond the allotted time, or that certain individuals dominate the discussion.

Step 3. Identify barriers that can prevent the team from operating consistently within the identified ideal norms. It might be that early meetings are subject to interference from traffic and unanticipated child care problems, or that less senior people in the group are reluctant to offer ideas when people in a position of authority are present.

Step 4. Gain agreement from all members of the group to engage in problem solving and modify norms that need strengthening. The group might agree not to schedule meetings prior to 9 AM or to rotate responsibility for presenting information at meetings so that all team members are heard.

By establishing and agreeing on team norms, the climate is set for the most effective functioning possible by team members. This exercise enables the group to overcome obstacles that typically interfere with productivity or job satisfaction and encourages involvement and investment on the part of each worker. It might be helpful as well to post the agreed upon norms at each meeting of the group to serve as a reminder of their commitment to the team process.

An essential defining feature of truly productive teams is individual willingness to support each other's agendas. Once again, the group is more effective than individuals functioning alone. One of the best examples I've ever observed of mutual support in a work group was in a small packaging and distribution company in the Midwest. Each member of the team was aware of the other members' responsibilities. Ongoing communication allowed them to know of any problem or crisis that arose. When

Steve in the shipping department was struggling to respond to four crucial orders at once and was concerned about not meeting his deadlines, two members of the reproduction and printing shop put their own tasks on hold for a few hours and pitched in to help him. It was interesting to note that they offered their help in a lively and upbeat manner and used humor to reduce the stress and tension that Steve was experiencing. When Irene's child care provider resigned suddenly and the interim arrangement required that she arrive at work later and leave early, members of her group picked up the slack for several weeks without being asked. Not only was this organization highly efficient in maintaining a consistent flow of work, but the level of personal satisfaction was high and turnover was rare.

This was the result of strong motivation on the part of the department head to create such an environment at the packaging company. He had made a major effort to create an atmosphere of trust and support. He also followed the classic example of being available for employees and recognizing their accomplishments as they occurred.

It is the simplest of assumptions that people's talents and abilities vary and assigning individuals to tasks they are good at is likely to result in a higher level of productivity. However, the issue goes beyond getting the job done and involves instilling in workers a powerful sense of value, accomplishment, and success. The effect is a deep psychological impact that has greater potential influence on the organization than basic productivity. People who have the opportunity to contribute to a team and feel valued for the unique gifts they bring are invested in the success of the team as a whole—whether a temporary work group or an ongoing effort.

If the experience of accomplishment is to be a solution to the present-day dilemma created by the lessening of promotions and advancements, then it is essential to understand ways to enable that accomplishment to occur. Accomplishment is a combination of feedback and confirmation that someone successfully achieved a certain goal as well as a feeling of fulfillment in attaining it. The latter aspect of accomplishment has a different effect than checking off a box or completing a task. It motivates the person to repeat the experience, resulting in higher levels of energy and momentum. In the context of a high-performing team the energy can be contagious, inspiring others to go beyond their potential as well. In the 1969 Super Bowl, when Joe Namath returned to the game to perform incredible feats—after receiving injuries that appeared to be game ending—his teammates responded with equally amazing performances. The result was not only a Super Bowl victory but a story that continues to inspire athletes 25 years later. This type of inspiration provides the impetus for ongoing individual and group achievement.

Accomplishment results from the efforts of individuals to seek activities that match their talents and abilities. It also comes from the recognition and appreciation of team members for the contribution made. We have all had the experience of struggling to generate energy for tasks that are difficult, boring, or not something we do well. And if our efforts go unappreciated it is even harder to sustain motivation. Generating a sense of accomplishment is a joint effort for which both individuals and groups share responsibility.

We have all heard of and experienced the positive effects of communication that is open, honest, and direct.

We instinctively know that it is easier to trust someone who is truthful and straight in their opinion of us and topics at hand. But why do we also see dishonesty and closed communication in groups we work with? Furthermore, what effect does closed communication have on commitments of high-performing teams? Open and direct communication is both a byproduct and a reinforcement of trust within groups. People are less open and direct when they are competing against each other than when they are functioning as a unit. No matter how talented and productive any individual on the team might be, if personal goals are not tied to an overall team commitment, territoriality and self-protectiveness might result in stifled communication. A perception that personal efforts are not valued by the group can also result in a disengaged, isolated mode of operating.

Another reason that people are reluctant to share ideas and feelings directly is fear of hurting or offending others. The problem this can create is that when people are offered only positive feedback there might be a perceived lack of genuineness, which further erodes trust. It is much healthier for team members to exchange more comprehensive feedback. This enhances credibility and confidence in each other. However, a certain level of skill and finesse is necessary for honesty and directness to be effective. It can be an excellent investment of time and resources to provide teams with professionally facilitated training in this area. Interpersonal skills training provides a safe forum for exchanging thoughts and feelings as well as an opportunity to acquire skills that can be used on a daily basis in the work setting.

Another characteristic of high-performance teams is an

investment in each other that goes beyond the walls and boundaries of the company. There is a commitment to understand, support, and nourish one another in ways that are not written or articulated in a formal manner. Mutually supportive workers inquire about others' family members, offering assistance with elder care or child care issues, going out of their way to make co-workers' lives a little easier. There also is a solid foundation of understanding. Members of the group know each other and stay abreast of events in their personal lives. They care about one another and share an esprit de corps that includes personal commitments as well. They support and encourage healthy behaviors like reducing weight or quitting smoking and offer this support in a nonjudgmental manner. In essence, members of high-performance teams share a commitment and loyalty to one another that extends beyond but significantly impacts the work setting.

Along with this type of reciprocal nurturing, it is typical to see the added benefit of enjoyment. People who are able to have fun together in the context of work will predictably have higher morale, lower absenteeism, and an increased level of motivation on the job. This camaraderie takes many forms and will be defined by the style of team members and the nature of the work setting. Co-workers might develop nicknames for each other, play practical jokes, give birthday parties for each other, or socialize after work. They find creative ways of incorporating fun and humor into the task at hand. Whatever form it takes, this dynamic serves to lighten the atmosphere and energizes the workplace.

What I have described in this section are the characteristics common to highly functional teams. However, it must be understood that few real-life work groups consistently display all of these characteristics. They are presented as an ideal vision that serves as a standard for the ultimate environment for group and individual commitments. Achieving these high standards of performance requires risk taking on the part of team members. Long-held values for independence and self- determination are not easily compromised. A real leap of faith is necessary if we are to place our fate, even in part, in the hands of others. All the evidence indicates, however, that these are risks worth taking. The price for playing it safe is work groups that function well below their potential and individuals who are understimulated, underrecognized, and underachieving.

▌ LEADERSHIP BEHAVIORS (MANAGER'S ROLE)

Considering the comprehensiveness and complexity of establishing and maintaining a high level of team and individual commitment can be a staggering thought to even the most ambitious of managers. However, just as there are ideal team behaviors, so are there ideal management behaviors to support team efforts. The following leadership Dos and Don'ts serve as workable parameters for the role of the manager in building team commitment.

▌ DON'T:

• *Overcontrol.* Many people in management positions feel compelled to check every detail, review and direct all aspects of work, and micromanage to a fault. Teams must have autonomy to be creative and productive. This does not eliminate the need for direction, but requires a shift of responsibility to allow the team to take risks, experience independence, and be trusted. Such action empowers the team, fuels motivation, and produces better results.

- *Motivate via head-to-head competition.* People respond to competitiveness differently. But placing workers in head-to-head competition is in essence pitting people against one another. For team performance, this is destructive.

- *Forget yourself.* Understand and attend to your own motivations, objectives, assets, and liabilities. Whether your role is the leader of the team or the person to whom the team leader answers, your own characteristics will impact the teamwork process.

▌ Do:

- *Create "solution space."* This term was coined by Tom Peters and Bob Waterman. Define the boundaries and scope of command that are clear, but give enough flexibility for personal input and group decision making. A certain amount of direction is necessary for teams to develop a course of action. Managers who fail to provide this will be seen as weak and ineffective. The ideal balance involves keeping people on course while allowing room to maneuver.

- *Give time and resource allocation.* Teams cannot achieve what they set out to do without adequate time and resources. Solid teamwork is less inclined to occur when you need a quick decision, when you need to rush a project through, or when you must get something done with as few resources as possible.

• *Reward team behavior.* Sounds simple enough, but some managers get focused on offering individual rewards for meeting performance goals. Even if certain team members are stars or need extra stroking, remember to highlight the achievements of the whole team, too. Don't let an overabundance of individual recognition outweigh the way the team is complimented as a whole.

• *Value different styles.* The more diverse a team, the greater the opportunity for a productive, complementary balance of skills and work styles. The emphasis here is not valuing "diversity" as in skin color, religion, or ethnicity, but noticing and working with the different ways team members communicate, decide, and complete tasks.

• *Have fun and enthusiasm in the workplace.* It can't be bought or manufactured, but it can be created through an ongoing sense of trust and closeness. One specific action a leader can take, however, is to maximize the potential for teams to build camaraderie in informal contexts. See what activities can be set up outside of work to build an informal sense of team among employees.

SUSTAINING TEAM PERFORMANCE

Bill Bradley once said, "Becoming number one is easier than remaining number one." Even when a team has achieved a workable balance of cooperation and cohesion and has performed exceptionally, the real challenge lies ahead. Like with any other accomplishment—whether it be losing 40 pounds, running a marathon, or being named number one sales team—sustaining team performance requires an ongoing adherence to the principles of commitment. Let's look at how each of the four cornerstones of commitment apply to teamwork.

█ VISION

It's a common mistake to establish vision and then assume it will stick. With teamwork, it's a requirement that there is regular revisiting of team vision and goals. Many teams report having the problem that interest and enthusiasm wanes as a result of slow momentum. The pace can be picked up through re-establishment of the vision. Another key component is being flexible about that vision, allowing it to be modified with changes that naturally occur.

One ideal way to keep people on task is to review objectives at regular intervals (monthly, quarterly, etc.) and involve team members in the refocusing process. This helps keep team members personally engaged. In addition, those team members who might stray with their own elements of a project, perhaps not benefitting the team as a whole, will be reined in. At all times, the team must remain aware of their direction, be accountable for the direction they have chosen, and maintain individual buy-in of that direction.

█ INSIGHT

Begin with what motivates members of the team. As discussed in Chapter 4, there are numerous ways of motivating people. The specific motivators will vary from person to person.

What do you know about the team's patterns of behavior? Most teams are able to describe what will happen as a predictable pattern of team development. Most people are familiar with the four stages that teams go through—Forming, Norming, Storming, and Performing. It is important, however, to anticipate developmental stages, such as Storming, and have a plan for dealing with them as they occur. As an example, it is fairly easy for teams to begin with a surge of energy and excitement and gradually lose momentum as problems arise and personal commitments to team effort falter. Team members who have experienced this can analyze the process and offer their own solutions.

Teams can also anticipate how the corporate culture might interfere with their efforts. This might include a cultural norm in which new ideas or priorities can override existing projects. If this is an established corporate culture norm, projects might never reach closure and people would feel as though they're left hanging. The team can decide whether to obey this norm and accept it as reality, or work for acceptable completion in spite of the norm.

ACCEPTANCE

Review the ACCEPT acronym in the context of team efforts:

A—Awareness or information that is relevant to the team's work. Keep an ongoing awareness of information that is needed and assign team members to the task of obtaining it. The group needs to be open to the idea of assimilating new information into their existing plan. Being open to new information is a characteristic of high functioning, flexible, and committed teams.

C—Control over what has to be done begins with each

individual on the team. It is also reflected in the attitude of the team. Decide what the team has control over and what they don't. This will keep the focus on achievable goals and free up the group's energy to be directed toward what can be achieved.

C—Choice. The concept of *full choice* must be understood and adhered to. Simply, it means that once a team member agrees to do something, he or she will be responsible for doing it, and more importantly, make the most of the decision and support it, not just endure it.

E—Efficacy: the belief that the team is capable of doing the job and that the outcome will be positive. When a team thinks optimistically, it is a self-fulfilling prophecy allowing them to leap over obstacles and challenges that would best a lesser team. One way to instill efficacy is to frequently cite the accomplishments of the team and compliment their efforts. This can't come from just the top; all team members should be inspired to give accolades to others.

P—People. Team solidarity will be enhanced when members are continuously asked for input and when their feelings and styles are considered by the team leader in the decision-making process.

T—Troubleshooting. Any successful team will have a method for dealing with problems and resolving conflict. Although there are many forms of such troubleshooting, some basic components any troubleshooting process should have are as follows:

1. Get input from all members on the source of the problem. These can be listed on a flip chart, or on individual sheets that are collected and summarized.

2. Do a root-cause analysis to condense the input into identifiable areas agreed upon by the group.

3. Brainstorm about ways to deal with the problem, without anyone questioning another's ideas or prejudging.

4. Select the top few solutions that: (a) have the most impact; (b) are most do-able; (c) are most practical; and (d) are most meaningful to the group's vision and goals.

5. Choose ways to implement the solutions.

INTEGRATION

Address inconsistencies as they arise. Don't wait for things to go away. Listen to what team members are saying, ask for clarification if there is confusion, and ensure that group members own their statements. Recognize and reward team and individual behaviors that lead to the successful attainment of the goals.

TEAMWORK PLUS

Using the four cornerstones to commitment in the teamwork context works in two ways: (1) it reinforces group efforts and (2) it provides better results, building commitment. At the same time, a foundation of stronger commitment results in more productive teamwork.

It's easy to see that teamwork progress and commitment are linked in important ways, and any team effort will benefit tremendously if commitment is the foundation.

Key Points in This Chapter

- Respecting and utlilzing each team member's unique capabilities benefit the team exponentially.

- Any high-performance team must have shared vision and shared accountability at its core.

- An essential defining feature of truly productive teams is individual willingness to support each other's agendas.

- Members of high-performance teams also have a commitment that goes beyond the walls and boundaries of the company.

9

PERSONAL COMMITMENTS

This chapter focuses on the application of the four factors of commitment to personal commitments—those goals and values that are distinctly individual and impact on quality of life both within and outside the work setting. The quality and strength of personal commitments are seen by many people as measures of integrity. Following through on behaviors that are important to our physical and psychological well-being demonstrates a healthy self-respect. Not doing so results in a drain on energy and low self-esteem. The same can be said for the promises we make to others. A promise becomes a commitment when we walk our talk—when we consistently do what we have said we will do.

It's rare to pick up a magazine or read the newspaper without coming across an article on the latest method for losing weight or on trimming your body using the latest breakthrough technology in fitness equipment. The accessibility of this type of information is enormous. Anyone interested in making a commitment to a health-related issue is not handicapped by a shortage of information, products, or services. The same holds true for other personal commitments, such as making the most of relationships, dealing with stress, or managing a career. The abudance of self-help books on the market is evidence of a significant need on the part of the general public. Assorted professional and paraprofessional opinions abound in attempts to cash in on this demand. Given this level of interest and the amount of information available, you would think that countless people would have successfully incorporated changes into their lives and sustained commitments to new ways of living. Unfortunately, the data do not support this. Here are some interesting facts reported in THE PREVENTION INDEX, a publication of *Prevention* magazine that reports on health trends in the U.S.:

• In 1994, nearly 7 out of 10 adults (68 percent) reported being overweight, **a 17 percent increase since 1983.**

• Slightly more than one-third (37 percent) of adults get regular exercise. This figure is **down 7 percent** from the previous year.

• Only about half (53 percent) of the people surveyed report that they avoid having too much fat in their diets, **down 8 percent** since 1989, and only 54 percent try to get enough fiber in their diets, **down 11 percent** in one year.

• A minority (40 percent) report trying to limit their consumption of sugar and sweet foods, a **22 percent decline** since 1983.

The only area where there is a strong sustained commitment to change health-related behaviors is that of safety: 73 percent report using seat belts all the time; 93 percent have smoke detectors in their homes; and 66 percent report never driving after drinking, which is up 27 percent since 1983.

The number of people reporting high levels of daily stress is **up 33 percent since 1985.**

Despite significant efforts to help people be more responsible and proactive in attending to one of the most important issues—health—there appears to be a *reverse* trend in motion. As a professional in the field of health promotion and as a psychologist, this trend is of great concern to me and was, in fact, one of the primary motivators behind my research into the concept of commitment.

One thing that stands out in reviewing this information is the fact that when behavior change involves a single task or behavior, such as installing a smoke alarm or fastening a seat belt, it seems to be easier to do. However, when a more complicated and demanding set of behaviors is involved and these behaviors have emotional and psychologic implications (such as losing weight or exercising regularly), a sustained level of success appears more difficult to achieve. *Comprehensive lifestyle changes are required, not simply isolated modifications of behavior.*

THE ROLE OF ORGANIZATIONAL SUPPORT

Let's take a step back and look at personal and work-related commitments from a big-picture perspective. We have already emphasized the fact that as business becomes leaner and more efficient, the average worker is asked to accomplish more in a shorter period of time. When this reality is combined with the additional demands of running a household and family, and transporting the kids to athletic events, music lessons, and other assorted activities, there are very few hours available for personal or leisure activities. This is especially true for single parents and two-career families. Now, consider what it takes to live healthier lifestyles: regular exercise, planning and preparing nutritious low-fat meals, taking time to unwind and manage stress. It becomes quite clear why we are seeing a reversal in health behaviors. Commitments that pay the bills will generally take precedence over those that enhance personal well-being and anything that requires significant time and effort will take a back seat to more urgent and pressing concerns. Part of the reason is our fast-paced society. For some people, though, "busyness" is an excuse not to lock into major efforts. Still others haven't learned to look at long-term goals and are inclined to focus on putting out daily fires rather than aim for a further, larger goal.

Working parents have often described to me the struggle to care for themselves in the context of lives that are already full of unfinished projects and incessant demands. When a child has been in day care for 10 hours already, it can be difficult to justify another hour or two to go to the gym, and at the end of a long and stressful work day, the fast food drive-up window looks much more appetizing than going home to slice, dice, and stir-fry—especially if you're slicing and dicing while toddlers are clinging to your legs, crying.

As a result, American workers continue to be overweight, stressed out, and at risk for a number of preventable illnesses. This takes a toll not only on individual well-being but on productivity and profits.

Adhering to personal commitments is essentially the same as adhering to work commitments. It involves applying the components of Vision, Insight, Acceptance, and Integration in a unified manner. It is crucial, however, not to overlook the potential impact of cultural and organizational supports that facilitate the process. Just as they can interfere with (or completely sabotage) personal commitments by placing increasing and sometimes unrealistic demands on people's time and energy, companies can choose to implement supportive programs and policies that enhance individual and family well-being.

Beginning in the 1980s we witnessed an interest on the part of organizations in people-friendly and family-friendly initiatives such as wellness programs, enhanced and expanded employee assistance programs, subsidized or on-site child care, flexible work arrangements, and even the availability of healthier foods in company cafeterias and vending machines. Unfortunately, except where there is strong evidence to support the fact that these kinds of efforts have a positive impact on the bottom line, they can easily get pushed aside in the face of economic pressures or an intensified pace in the workplace.

It is advisable, therefore, to explore the impact of initiatives such as these in a practical and strategic context. One of the leading resources in this arena is Work/Family Directions, Boston, Massachusetts. In a recent business symposium entitled "Recommitting the Workforce," Fran Rodgers, CEO of Work/Family Directions, brought together business leaders, health care professionals, researchers, and service providers to discuss the following two questions, both of which have been addressed throughout this book:

1. As companies find promises of long-term job security, steady career growth, and ever-increasing salaries unrealistic in the face of intense competition and a fast-changing business environment, what can they offer in their place to earn employees' commitment?

2. With an increasingly diverse workforce pushed to ever higher performance standards in the face of growing insecurity, how can companies draw out the creative energies of their employees?

Among the most significant themes and ideas considered at the meeting were benefits and supports that address employees' most important personal and family needs, and employee health and wellness. It is a safe assumption that employees will perform better under circumstances where they feel that their lives outside work are respected, and when their employer comes through on the issues that matter to them.

The Families and Work Institute found that workers who had more flexible time and leave options and more dependent-care benefits feel more loyal to their employers and are more committed to helping their employers succeed. In addition, it was determined by the Institute's research that workers with more job autonomy and control over their work schedules are less burned out by their work, take more initiative at work, and plan to remain with their current employer longer than other workers.

A recent study determined that employees of organizations with nonsupportive work and family policies report nearly double the rate of burnout (54 percent as opposed to 27 percent) and experience twice the incidence of stress-related illnesses. Among people experiencing difficulties with child care, 62 percent said they would consider leaving their jobs for a position that offered more flexible work arrangements.

When we consider the fact that only 10 percent of families now have a parent at home attending to the needs of children, it becomes clear that almost all employees are affected by dependent-care issues. Today's workers are feeling the pressure of balancing demanding jobs with family and self-care. They are no longer as willing to sacrifice their personal lives on the altar of a company's business objectives. It is an interesting fact that, according to several studies, between half and two-thirds of workers (both men and women) would work for less money in order to have more personal and family time.

The assumption that employees in today's economy are so grateful to have jobs at all that they will do anything to keep them is a faulty one. This change in values must be recognized by companies that hope to retain valuable workers and maximize their productivity. Particularly in the context of modern technology, with the availability of fax machines, conference calling, and advanced information systems, the old work rules and schedules are outmoded and can be discouraging and frustrating to employees. It is no longer necessary to restrict people to a rigid eight-hour (or ten- or twelve-hour) work day, or even to doing their work in a particular setting. As I discussed in Chapter 7, however, the organizational culture, from the CEO down to front-line supervisors, must support family-friendly guidelines for those policies to be effective. It accomplishes nothing for companies to offer flexible policies if employees are afraid to use them. Although workers are desperate for flexibility and are even willing to leave their company to get it, few will take advantage of such programs if they are not offered with respect.

In another significant study, two-thirds of working women surveyed reported that they needed more flexibility *in order to do a better job*. However, more than half of the managers and professional men stated a belief that a request for flexibility indicated *a lack of seriousness about the job.* When leaders and managers fail to recognize the relationship between people's individual commitments to their careers and to their personal lives and their loyalty to an organization, everyone loses.

The same principle applies to health-related commitments. It is unfortunate that efforts within companies to support healthy behaviors and to take preventive approaches to health issues are sometimes viewed by managers as a superfluous or an unnecessary expenditure of resources. In reality, the evidence is strong that it is much less costly to prevent illness than it is to cure it. Companies such as Johnson and Johnson, AT&T, Texas Instruments, Tenneco, and Adolph Coors, to mention just a few, have demonstrated not only a significant return on dollars invested in wellness programs, but reductions in absenteeism and reported work stress, and increases in morale and job satisfaction.

SOCIAL AND CULTURAL CHANGE

Another important perspective on personal commitments is the frame of reference provided by addressing the rapid and pervasive social changes that have occurred within the last generation. Most American workers live in a very different world from their parents', and commitments to careers, families, relationships, and health behaviors have sustained damage and loss as a result. As discussed previously, many of these changes are (or have the potential to be) positive.

Dramatic shifts in social roles that in the past limited

both women and men to gender-specific tasks and responsibilities have broadened our perceptions of career and family values. Leaner organizations have encouraged a greater degree of self-responsibility along with a more highly evolved vision of work identity, and technologic advances have provided us with a level of convenience and access to information that would have been unimaginable a generation ago.

As we look at individuals and their personal commitments to core values such as relationships, work identity, and health, this backdrop of tremendous change takes on a particular significance. The stress of adapting to such profound transformations is, in and of itself, an issue for concern. More specifically, however, until we are able to more clearly define new roles and redefine both organizational and social cultures, the confusion and conflict that naturally occur in times of major change will continue to complicate not only family life and marriages, but individuals' physical and mental health.

A further source of conflict and confusion lies in the influence of media and advertising on our perceptions of ourselves and our roles. We are all subject on a daily basis to a barrage of messages and images, many of which, for the purpose of selling products, are idealized, distorted, or even downright silly. Our children clamor for a variety and quantity of toys, video games, and articles of clothing that are far beyond what most of us ever possessed or even aspired to possess while growing up. (Many of the items now considered basic necessities by our kids didn't even exist when our parents had the responsibility of providing for us.)

Advertisements for everything from household appliances to automobiles depict attractive, energetic, smiling, fit and trim people successfully juggling careers and families while apparently experiencing no significant stress whatsoever. And if they should develop a "tension headache" or come down with a virus, all that is required to return things to normal is the appropriate capsule or tablet because they "haven't got time for the pain." These images, in an insidious and powerful way, make it even more difficult for today's working people to develop realistic and achievable visions and sustain the motivation to pursue and maintain their commitments. With the media as a prominent source of standards and shaper of norms in our society, it is crucial that we evaluate the impact of messages emphasizing perfectionism, quick fixes, and immediate gratification. All these concepts are counterconducive to sustained, meaningful commitments.

COMMITMENT TO PERSONAL VALUES

Without exception, every person I have worked with, whether in the context of health promotion, teaching, or psychotherapy, has expressed the same core values of *relationships, physical and mental health,* and a sense of *meaning and purpose* in their lives (frequently related to work or career).

In fact, a primary motivator for people to seek out therapy, education, or information related to health behaviors is the conflict and pain that result when these values are compromised. The four factors of commitment serve as an effective foundation for refocusing and centering on the things that are truly important to people, and for sustaining lifestyles and behaviors that support them.

The Commitment Factor Profile is an effective tool for assessing the strength of personal commitments and identifying areas where change or additional support might be needed. It is advisable to refer to Chapter 2 as a beginning point when addressing individual values and goals.

In the past 12 years I have conducted over 500 workshops, seminars, and classes on various health enhancement programs, including smoking cessation, weight management, cholesterol reduction, fitness, and general well-being. In doing these workshops, I have noticed a predictable pattern of commitment behaviors. It is most common for people to complete wellness programs fired up, enthusiastic, and demonstrating all of the needed thoughts, words, and actions of a truly committed individual. Then, after approximately two months, things begin to deteriorate. After three months, only 25 to 30 percent of the participants are still fairly committed. This phenomenon is also evident in the 1988 Surgeon General's landmark report on nicotine addiction, in which Dr. C. Everett Koop illustrates a similar relapse rate for people addicted to cigarettes, heroine, and alcohol. All these addicted individuals, after intensive treatments, show almost identical drop-off rates of 70 percent, and a leveling off of this percentage at 12 months.

This struck me as an interesting parallel in behavior change and pure evidence of the difficulty in maintaining adjustment to new ways of living (lifestyle). It also reaffirms how the great majority of people will resort to old behaviors, even when those behaviors might be life threatening.

Lifestyle also plays a part in relationship commitments, and it's not uncommon to hear couples reporting marital distress resulting from incompatible lifestyles. The very first couple I saw for marital counseling demonstrated this. This young couple had been married for two years and were experiencing problems that led them to question whether or not to stay in the relationship. When asked about their lifestyle and what their expectations for living together were, they had quite different views. He wanted to live in the city in a high-rise condo with no pets and frequent nights out for dinner and socializing. Her desired lifestyle was a large home in the country, multiple pets (and children), and nights at home alone together.

My first thoughts were, How did these two get together? and Why didn't they talk about these things before making their vows? When I inquired about the history of their relationship, they reported having known each other only three months before getting married, and they didn't remember having any detailed discussions about where or how they would live. Now that the "honeymoon" was over, they were left with the reality of a shared life, but conflicting visions and major differences in values. I have seen the same kind of issues come into play with regard to career and life purpose commitments. Many couples have not had childhood experiences that prepared them adequately for supporting each others' career aspirations. In the traditional families of the past, with their well-defined but separate roles designated by gender, it might have been easier for successful families to provide reciprocal and mutual support.

Today's couples often feel as though their respective work roles place them in competition with one another, in their needs for free time, child care, assistance with domestic responsibilities, and emotional support. Families who are able to successfully negotiate a balance will be better equipped to adapt to change and manage stress, and are likely to be more effective in achieving a variety of personal goals and commitments.

Let's examine two significant personal values/commitments in more detail.

█ RELATIONSHIPS

It will be interesting to see what percentage of the baby boomers will celebrate 50th wedding anniversaries in the future, or what the average number of marriages will be per person in the year 2000. A large crop of disillusioned people are struggling to resolve conflicts with changing roles. In many cases, people have had painful personal experiences with their parents' divorces and/or their own. As a result, they are waiting longer to marry or avoiding marriage altogether. A number of those who *are* willing to risk a commitment to a lifelong, monogamous relationship find it very difficult to sustain in the context of complicated, stressful lives and uncertainty about individual roles and responsibilities.

The array of complexities that social change has introduced into our lives, combined with the ever-increasing pace at which many of us function, can easily cloud our focus and make it difficult to stay centered on our commitments. I have worked with many two-career families who consistently report the same kinds of struggles. Typically, the basic responsibilities of feeding, clothing, transporting, and nurturing children, along with domestic chores such as paying bills, shopping for food, doing laundry, and other household tasks, are not only a daunting challenge to complete during the few hours left to people outside of work, but are often a source of conflict between couples as well.

Simply deciding who does what and when is a process that many of our parents didn't have to address. When we add to this the fact that people often don't have time to get sufficient sleep (a recent study indicated that two-thirds of American adults are chronically sleep deprived) much less relax and enjoy leisure time, it is easy to see how marital intimacy gets put on the back burner. Unfortunately, without the necessary time and attention, a marriage can't grow strong enough to withstand the pressures placed on it by modern life. I encourage couples to re-think their priorities and keep them in the foreground via daily communication and scheduled time alone together (although this usually means letting the soccer game or the laundry take a backseat on occasion). Continually re-fining and reinforcing a shared vision of the relationship, and being willing to accept the sacrifices required to attend to it, are necessary for a sustained commitment. In addition, insight into past relationship problems, and an understanding of each person's needs and personality are essential for true and lasting intimacy.

Finally, the much-used phrase, walking your talk, applies in a profound way to relationships. Paying lip service to how important someone is to us or how much we love him or her means very little if we don't demonstrate it through our behavior by consistently supporting, affirming, and *enjoying* him or her.

Parenting is another relationship commitment that has become increasingly complex and difficult to sustain in today's world. Once again, changing roles and a faster pace of living serve to complicate the challenge. A woman I worked with in therapy had significant guilt and feelings of inadequacy following the birth of her first child. She had waited until she was into her 30s to become a mother and had, in the meantime, established a meaningful career as a human resource manager. Her discomfort centered around the frustration and stress she experienced as she adjusted her work schedule to a part-time arrangement in order to be at home two days a week with her daughter. In addition to the predictable conflicts between her job and her responsibilities to her child, the woman was surprised and extremely guilty about the fact that she often felt bored, aggravated, helpless, and unappreciated when she spent days at home with the toddler.

As we explored her expectations (her *vision*) going into motherhood, she began to develop insight into several factors that had combined to produce her current level of unhappiness. First of all, like many new parents, she had had a somewhat unrealistic view of what motherhood would be like. Many of us have been socialized to believe that nurturing children is something that comes easily and naturally to all women and that provides them with ongoing gratification and pleasure. Realistically, this is not always the case. In reality, parenting is often frustrating and tedious, despite the profound rewards it provides. Particularly for people who have become accustomed to a certain level of status and appreciation for their work, and to a work environment that allows for a high degree of control and accomplishment, the demands of caring for children can be extremely difficult to adapt to.

Once these realities were acknowledged, my client was able to define a more realistic vision of herself as a mother, one that capitalized on her unique strengths rather than setting a standard that she couldn't attain. This allowed her to let go of her guilt for feeling some very normal conflict and stress. An additional challenge she faced was the relaxing of her standards with regard to housekeeping, which were based on memories of her mother's style of functioning in a traditional full-time, at-home role.

Fathers are also in the process of redefining their commitments to parenthood. Men in the current generation of parents are faced with the unique challenge of trying to become more involved with their children than their fathers were and assume more domestic responsibilities while having significantly less discretionary time in which to do them. Finding creative ways to build and sustain powerful bonds with our children in the context of extremely busy lives is not easy, but it is possible. Once again, it begins with a new vision that is realistic and workable.

I've talked to a number of fathers who are discovering that, rather than trying to engage their children through scheduled activities, such as baseball games or trips to the zoo or museum (the best-laid plans of fathers are unfortunately often subject to interference from unexpected work demands, illness, or a toddler's need to nap), it is more effective and practical to connect with them at brief, but frequent intervals by sharing jokes, silly nicknames, or simple, but meaningful rituals such as a foot massage at bedtime or a piggyback ride to the bathtub.

Older children can be made to feel valued and attended to by asking their opinion on anything from current events to what to have for dinner. The important thing is to remain focused on the importance of staying connected to our children and to consistently look for opportunities to do so. Significant memories are often of small and simple things.

Whether the relationship is marital, parent-child or another significant bond, the idea is to use the factors of Vision, Acceptance, Insight, and Integration as a basis for making relationship commitments a high priority, and maintaining them in ways that enhance our well-being.

HEALTH BEHAVIORS

The same influences of social change and the media have had a profound impact on individuals' commitments to health behaviors. First of all, we are dealing with an entirely new definition of health and how to achieve and maintain it. The role of regular exercise, the influence of stress, and the way in which we measure healthy nutrition are all relatively new and often somewhat confusing concepts to integrate. And, as we have described, simply finding the time to incorporate these goals into an increasingly complicated and fast-paced style of living presents a major challenge.

Unrealistic visions of a sculpted physique or smooth cellulite-free thighs (based on images in television commercials or popular magazines) can be discouraging to people who want to pursue improved physical fitness. Even the most well-intentioned experts in the field can present us with goals that we are unlikely to achieve, much less maintain. I have witnessed dietitians and exercise physiologists talking to groups about the importance of 45 minutes of intensive aerobic exercise five to seven times per week, and presenting a disdainful attitude toward any consumption of highly processed or fast foods. Often these professionals were young, single, and/or childless and worked in environments that were highly supportive of their healthy lifestyles. What they failed to understand was that the average working person with a family lives in very different circumstances, and is therefore more likely to be discouraged than to be motivated by such instruction.

It is necessary for each of us to define a manageable and realistic lifestyle vision before we can generate the motivation to pursue health behavior commitments. For example, recent research supports the fact that a 10-minute brisk walk every other day can actually have a significant positive impact on our well-being. This is a goal that most people find reasonable and possible to do. An understanding that we might have to give up some things (relax our perfectionistic standards, simplify our schedules, or discipline ourselves to eat less fat and sugar) must be part of the picture as well. It is also advisable to explore individual preferences and patterns of behavior in order to understand what motivates each of us, and define a healthy lifestyle that works on an ongoing basis. Health behaviors must be viewed as components of a comprehensive approach to living—a way of *being* to which we are fully committed.

THE ROLE OF DISRUPTIVE COGNITIVE STYLES IN PERSONAL COMMITMENTS

Various influences come into play as well when we explore faltering personal commitments. The disruptive cognitive styles discussed in Chapter 6 have a role in individual success and failure, as well as work-related goals.

For example, when an individual is prone to denial, it's understandable he or she they might interpret health-related information that is inconsistent or controversial to support a lack of positive action. The recent research indicating that margarine might not be more beneficial than butter in the war against heart disease might generate the notion, nobody really knows what is good or bad for you anyway, so why alter your diet at all? In this case, despite the fact that reducing fat in the diet *is* universally advocated, conflicting or confusing information is used to absolve the denier of responsibility for doing so.

Recent efforts to restrict smoking in the workplace are being met with strong contention on behalf of smokers. It is interesting to consider that this resistance might actually have less to do with a perceived violation of personal freedom than with the *oppositional* cognitive style of the individuals involved. Those same people might well choose to *voluntarily* abstain from smoking in other contexts (such as in a church or in a friend's new car) where they don't feel that they are being told what to do.

The startling reality that more than 95 percent of all people who lose significant amounts of weight through formal treatment programs or diets regain the weight within a year is testimony to the *externalized* thinking of many of the participants. The expectation that a temporary program or diet will take the place of ongoing lifestyle change is externalized thinking in its truest form.

When Oprah Winfrey rolled out her red wagon of fat onto the stage after a major weight loss via a liquid diet, I mentioned that to weight reduction groups as an example of what *not* to do.

More recently, Oprah Winfrey has attested to the fact that only through regular exercise and low-fat eating was she able to lose the weight she regained after going off the liquid diet, and that she now has a true and ongoing dedication to being fit and healthy, not just thinner. Like many other people who have repeatedly lost and gained unwanted excess weight, her sustained success required a more comprehensive and integrated commitment, and an approach to health that relied on personal accountability, not a program or diet plan.

The continuing 50 percent divorce rate might well be indicative of a belief that repairing a damaged relationship or making a life-long promise is too overwhelming or complicated.

This discouraged type of thinking often leads to abandoning relationship commitments and giving in to yet another failure.

CLARIFYING AND REFINING GOALS

In my experience with people trying to improve their lives in any of these areas, I have found that people are most likely to be successful if they focus on one major commitment at a time. Attempting to stop smoking, reduce blood cholesterol, lose weight, begin an exercise program, and improve marital intimacy all at the same time is an obvious setup for failure. It is also true, however, that various personal goals can impact on each other in both positive and negative ways. Being healthier often gives us more energy and a positive outlook that can enhance our relationships, and family support is crucial for sustaining health behavior commitments.

In contrast, the time we wish to devote to exercise or career goals might sometimes interfere with marital or family time—or vice versa. This is why continually clarifying and refining our commitment visions and evaluating the strength and viability of our personal goals is so important. The four factors of commitment can assist us in achieving and maintaining balance, satisfaction, and a sense of power and purpose in our lives.

Key Points in This Chapter

- Adhering to personal commitments is the same as adhering to work commitments.

- Influences of social change and the media have had a profound impact on individuals' commitment to health behaviors.

- Denial discouraged, externalized and oppositional thinking can restrict efforts to reach a goal.

10

Committing to Commit

Commitment, as I have described it in this book, is not a temporary behavior change to remedy a short-term problem, nor is it an agreement to placate and silence a person who is asking for something to be changed. Temporary agreements are easy. Committing to major change takes effort and time, and it is often daunting to anticipate a long-term comprehensive challenge. Sometimes getting started is the most difficult part of the journey. Beginning with a certain amount of dissatisfaction about the present state makes it easier to move through the stages and master the commitment.

This book is not intended for the person looking for a quick solution or a temporary fix for personal or organizational problems. It also is not appropriate for someone who is content with the status quo and only marginally interested in improving things. This book is for those who want to be more consistent in doing things that they set out to do, who want to experience greater satisfaction in doing them, and who are receptive to the challenge of ongoing improvement in their lives.

Moving through the sequential order of the four factors of commitment makes it easier to sustain commitments. Ascending from vision to insight and then to acceptance will make it possible to become integrated and committed. As discussed, commitments that involve important values require a great deal of change in our attitudes, behaviors, and relationships with people. This change is automatically met with resistance, especially in times when we are called upon to do more and at a faster pace.

In addition to the four factors of commitment, there is another element that affects the process. Without it, commitment of any kind is likely to get off to a sluggish start and will lack energy and momentum. This element is *dissatisfaction*.

▌ WHY DISSATISFACTION IS A PLACE TO BEGIN

Perhaps it's the nature of my business or maybe it's a simple reality of the way I've seen people go about making changes in their lives, but in my experience, commitment begins with a need to change something that is causing discomfort or dissatisfaction. This dissatisfaction might be something that comes from an outside source (you must make the commitment to keep your job or to stay in a relationship), or it might come from a need to improve one's life (commit to a college education or to learn a particular skill). Whatever the source of the change, the resulting feeling of dissatisfaction or threat can initiate the process. I have observed this in people suffering the consequences of alcoholism, who superficially think that they don't have a problem with drinking (they're satisfied with the way things are), but when confronted with losing their family or job, begin to explore how unhappy they are with their lives. It is then that they begin to contemplate changes.

In my professional experience, frequently the impetus for beginning lifestyle changes is a heightening of consciousness related to something that is wrong with the present state of affairs. It might come in the form of a serious diagnosis, such as emphysema or a heart attack that motivates someone to quit smoking or begin exercise, or it might be something as simple as no longer being able to zip up a favorite pair of trousers. This discomfort or anxiety, the *dissatisfaction with the way things are,* provides the spark that ignites the fire of commitment genesis.

I have also seen this phenomenon in work groups who vehemently resist reorganization or downsizing efforts and want things to remain as they are (satisfied). However, when they face the reality of the present structure or the way they currently do business, the dissatisfaction that emerges helps them to accept the pending (and necessary) changes. Although the unfaltering optimist in me is always ready to search for the positive in any situation, I have grown to recognize how a certain amount of dissatisfaction can aid the commitment process, especially when sacrifices have to be made.

Here's an example of how commitments can be influenced by dissatisfaction. I worked with a group of engineers and draftsmen whose department was being downsized and reorganized. This was occurring for the typical reason: to cut costs. Most of the participants in the workshop, entitled "Dealing with Change," had been with the company for many years and were distressed over pending changes. Emotions ran high in the session, and I became aware of the fact that they were holding on for dear life. In hearing their story it also *seemed* that these people were content with their jobs and didn't see a need to change things.

When I explored the possible reasons for the changes being made and asked them to look at the rationale behind the changes, they began to present a different picture. Things were far from perfect in the organization. Many of them were, in fact, unhappy with the support they were receiving (equipment was outdated and cumbersome), and they recognized the efficiencies that a new computerized format could offer. They also saw that they were overstaffed, with some of them commenting on the boredom and frustration of downtime.

The time spent on analysis of the present state was well worth the effort. It helped the group to move forward. I realized that the majority of the workers were not able to formalize a vision because of the distorted perception of contentment they held. When they shifted their attention to overcoming problems in their work setting and spent time on evaluating themselves, they experienced a lessening of resistance and an openness to accepting change.

The caveat here is that in dealing with resistance in the early stages of commitment, it is necessary to raise consciousness by reevaluating the environment and individual perceptions before proceeding to establish vision. It is important to remember that resistance to change is normal and not to be frustrated by it. Identifying and exploring dissatisfaction with the present is not about negativity or discouragement. It is simply an objective assessment of why change is a good idea.

SETBACKS TO WATCH FOR

Though information from this book can be applied to a variety of situations, there will be pitfalls along the way that need further exploration. Almost all commitments experience a brief lapse in clarity as other priorities come into view. It takes extra effort to work through that lack of clarity and stick with the vision. A healthy vision is more than an idealized one. It's a realistic future view that anticipates ups and downs and adjusts its course based on experience.

Another potential setback might occur because of inertia. The law of inertia states that an object in motion has a tendency to stay in motion and an object at rest has a tendency to remain at rest. Remaining on a roll will strengthen and reinforce. However, there will be times when that action will stop. The challenge at these times is to resist the temptation to give in to procrastination, delay, or temporary abandonment of your commitment, thinking that you will get to it tomorrow. Although a temporary hiatus helps from time to time, keeping pace is often much easier than starting again. To overcome inertia, make an agreement with yourself not to talk yourself into or out of commitment behaviors. This might require putting yourself into automatic pilot from time to time, and not think about whether or not to do it.

My wife's approach to exercise demonstrates this technique clearly. After a long day of work, she has learned from experience that she will relieve stress and be energized if she goes for a run. She also knows that if she hesitates at all, she probably won't do it (my wife refers to the principle of inertia as the tendency for an object in motion to remain in motion and an object at rest on the couch with potato chips to remain on the couch with the chips). She lays out sweats and shoes in the morning and proceeds directly from the car to the bedroom and out the front door without stopping to engage in any contemplation about whether or not to run. This is sustaining momentum in a very literal sense.

Another word of caution: do not overdepend on others or outside sources. All of us are prone to frustration and discouragement when others fail to provide the support or understanding we need. At these times our commitments are challenged. Whether it's a boss who forgets to mention your contributions to team accomplishment or a spouse who fails to comment on your weight loss, you don't need to experience a setback as a result. Support is a necessary, but insufficient condition for sustaining commitments. Tap into the power of your *own* commitment first and foremost.

Also, remember that relapse prevention strategies can help overcome commitment abandonment by determining what did not work and why. This will also enhance self-efficacy, which is at the core of sustained commitments. From the outset, any commitment goal must be accompanied by a plan to maintain the commitment as well as to achieve some level of performance.

█ What Managers Need to Consider

For managers interested in using these commitment-building concepts, there are also a few questions that must be addressed. As with any new training program, initiative, or corporate directive, there are often large gaps between knowledge, intentions, and actions. The manager should pause for a moment and consider:

1. After reading this book, is it likely that I will change the way I relate to people I work with?

2. What would it take for me to change the way I do the things I do and incorporate commitment-building strategies?

Just as thinking processes can impede acquisition of personal commitments, they can also result in a thought by the manager that these things will never work. A manager choosing to implement strategies to build commitment should watch out for his own thoughts that inhibit commitment, such as:

- This is too complicated. I don't have the time.

- I have tried things like this before and they never work.

- How can I build commitments in an organization that doesn't care about people?

- Making commitments is a personal thing. I can't control people's lives.

- I'm no psychologist. I haven't been trained to do these things.

- This is a training issue and the training department should be doing this, not me.

This type of thinking creates roadblocks. Even if a situation looks similar to efforts tried before, every experience is different. It's important to question the validity of statements like the ones above because they are merely mental setups on the part of the manager to create failure. It takes self-responsibility, the knowledge gained from past unsuccessful efforts, and a strong belief in a successful outcome.

If a manager is to take on the challenge of building a

committed workforce, it must begin with a strong base of self-efficacy. When a manager takes the position that there are too many forces affecting employee commitment and dealing with these issues is too complicated, achievements will undoubtedly be compromised by self-doubt. As a result, the commitment to facilitate commitments doesn't have the impetus to succeed.

Many of the strategies and suggestions I've offered here are not recommendations that are foreign to the manager; it is likely that they are already part of his or her repertoire. The key, however, is to assess current management practices compared to what is presented in this book, and determine areas of strength and areas that need improvement.

One manager I consulted with professed a belief in survival of the fittest when it came to commitments, and said she believed that those who didn't meet their commitments would soon be out of work. This perspective not only removes the manager from active support and involvement in employee's commitments (personal and work-related), but the manager also runs the risk of being adversarial. In times of high work stress, today's manager cannot afford to alienate and disenfranchise fellow employees or subordinates. In fact, a survey of AT&T employees indicated that the number one predictor of high employee stress was a nonsupportive manager.

The interested manager is responsive to basic ways of facilitating commitments. The following guidelines will help:

• Listen to the needs, goals, and desires of employees. Allow individuals to share their concerns and conflicts with you before offering advice or support.

- Summarize what you are hearing and check it out to be sure you are understanding accurately.

- Distinguish between personal and work commitments and ask, Is your work being affected by personal commitments? (And vice versa.)

- Set goals and identify support mechanisms that you both agree to. Revise goals as needed.

- Share responsibility and accountability for meeting agreed-upon commitments.

- Keep the individual focused on commitments through empowerment and delegation.

- Develop a problem-solving approach and use it with the individual regularly to deal with conflict.

- Be patient. In dealing with commitments you are dealing with complicated life issues.

There are also things to watch out for and avoid:

- Steer clear of the temptation to tell people what they should be doing, especially when it comes to personal commitments. Don't lecture or teach.

- Don't penalize a lack of success or shortcomings without problem solving first. Demonstrate that commitment building involves learning from setbacks and incorporating this learning into the overall plan.

- Don't *excessively* reassure and praise accomplishments. This creates a lack of authenticity.

THE ORGANIZATION'S ROLE

An organization committed to building commitments will demonstrate the principles outlined in this book and will carry out the process on all levels. It begins at the top of the organization, with senior executives who articulate their personal commitments to the company vision *in writing*. Once they are formulated, each successive level of management will then outline its commitments based on those expressed by the level above it. Collectively, all employees' objectives then form the foundation that supports the company's overriding mission, which translates into a greater potential for winning in the workplace.

This fully integrated approach also becomes the basis for a performance appraisal system that personally ties each individual into company objectives and establishes measures that everyone can relate to. When individuals are able to see how they fit into the big picture, their sense of contribution and belonging is enhanced and they have a clearer understanding of the strategic linkage between their own performance and the success of the company as a whole. With a commitment-based approach, it is also possible to provide informal feedback and evaluation. It is no longer necessary or appropriate to wait for a yearly appraisal session to determine the extent to which results match commitments. In fact, with accomplishment as a key driver, informal feedback sessions with supporting managers can become markers that are anticipated and valued. For organizational cultures to improve and develop, this is a necessary process.

This new perspective will lay the foundation for involvement and will instill the understanding of what it is like to truly be part of a team. A sense of team also requires that the organization go beyond the traditional work contract and touch people's personal lives. Consideration of and respect for family and social (community) issues, and collaboration on how to meet personal needs are evidence of a truly committed company. Major endeavors must extend beyond the short-term focus of quarterly or annual performance. If we ever hope to restore the feeling of security that once generated company loyalty—that sense of being part of a family—organizations must commit to understanding and reintegrating family values into the world of work. Companies that are able to rediscover and create a true spirit of community will be the leaders of the 21st century. Business must become more than just buildings and profit margins. It has to nurture and honor the human element that is the essence of our highest purpose.

It's important to keep in mind that commitment building is a shared responsibility and that the potential payoff is for the manager and the company, as well as the employee. This win/win scenario creates the environment for high performance, emotional and psychologic well-being, and a team spirit that will make the difference between *wanting to* and *having to* be there.

Inspiring commitment takes time and effort, but when a manager does achieve it, the results are stellar. Each employee, no matter what his or her position or number of years of service, can learn to display the dedication all managers and companies want: a personal excitement akin to that of being a new, enthusiastic employee, eager for a challenge, ready to channel his or her unique talents and interests into playing an integral role in the work process.

Appendix

ASSESSMENT TOOLS FOR MANAGING STRESS
AND BUILDING TEAMWORK

Assessment Tools for Managing Stress and Building Teamwork

COPING INVENTORY FOR STRESSFUL SITUATIONS (CISS)

Norman Endler and James Parker

Adolescent, Adult

Purpose: Measures coping styles in individuals.

Description: 48-item paper-pencil or computer-administered instrument measuring three major types of coping styles: Task Oriented, Emotion Oriented, and Avoidance Coping. The CISS also identifies two types of Avoidance Coping patterns: Distraction and Social Support. Scores provide a profile of an individual's coping strategy. Adult and adolescent forms available. Self-administered. Suitable for group use.

Scoring: Carbonized scoring forms; may be computer scored.

Cost: Kit (test manual, 25 Quik Score forms) $29.00; IBM PC compatible version (50 administrations and scorings) contact publisher for cost.

Publisher: Multi-Health Systems Inc.

COPING OPERATIONS PREFERENCE ENQUIRY (COPE)

Will Shutz

Adult

Purpose: Measures individual preference for certain types of coping or defense mechanisms, used for counseling and therapy.

Description: 6-item paper-pencil test measuring the characteristic use of five defense mechanisms: denial, isolation, projection, regression-dependency, and turning-against-the-self. Each item describes a person and his behavior in a particular situation. The respondent rank orders five alternative ways a person might feel: the alternatives represent the inventory's five coping mechanisms. Materials include separate forms for men and women. May be self-administered; however, an examiner is recommended. Suitable for group use.

Scoring: Examiner evaluated

Cost: 25 tests (specify male or female) $15.75.

Publisher: Consulting Psychologists Press, Inc.

Assessment Tools for Managing Stress and Building Teamwork

COPING RESOURCES INVENTORY (CRI)

Allen L. Hammer and M. Susan Marting

Adult

Purpose: Measures an individual's resources for coping with stress. Used in individual counseling, workshops, and health settings.

Description: 60-item paper-pencil inventory consisting of five scales, measuring an individual's cognitive, social physical, emotional, and values resources. The results identify the resources a person has developed for coping with stress and those that still must be developed. The manual includes scale descriptions, reliability and validity information, separate norms for males and females, and case illustrations for interpreting the profiles. Examiner required. Suitable for group use.

Scoring: Hand key; may be computer scored

Cost: Manual $9.00; score keys $10.00; 25 test booklets $8.00; 10 prepaid answer sheets $36.00; 50 non-prepaid answer sheets $22.00; 50 profiles $12.50.

Publisher: Consulting Psychologists Press, Inc.

COPING STRATEGIES SCALES (COSTS)

E. Edward Beckham and Russell Adams

Adult—Ages 18 and older

Purpose: Assesses the coping strategies used by individuals who are depressed or under stress. Used by researchers and clinicians.

Description: 142-item paper-pencil multiple-choice questionnaire assessing coping strategies along 10 dimensions. An SAS computer-scoring program is available free of charge. Self-administered. Suitable for group use. Available in French.

Scoring: Hand key; may be computer scored

Cost: Free

Publisher: E. Edward Beckham, Ph.D.

Assessment Tools for Managing Stress and Building Teamwork

JOB STRESS INDEX (JSI)

Bonnie A. Sandman and Patricia C. Smith

Adult

Purpose: Assess various aspects of job stress of employed adults.

Description: Paper-pencil attitude questionnaire divided into 11 subtests. Subtests include Lack of Feedback, Lack of Participation, Lack of Achievement, Time Pressure, Lack of Interpersonal Skills of Supervisor, Lack of Competence of Supervisor, Lack of Interpersonal Skills of Others, Lack of Competence of Others, Red Tape, Job Insecurity, and Physical Demands and Danger. Items are answered in a "yes-no-sometimes" format. Scores are obtained for each subtest, yielding a profile of employee attitudes. A 6th-grade reading level is required. Self-administered. Suitable for group use.

Scoring: May be hand scored; computer scoring available from publisher.

Cost: 100 booklets $92.00

Publisher: Smith, Sandman & McCreery

MANAGEMENT BURNOUT SCALE

John W. Jones and Donald M. Moreitti

Adult

Purpose: Assesses burnout or work stress among managerial-level employees.

Description: Multiple-item paper-pencil test assessing burnout or work stress through four types of factors: cognitive reactions, affective reactions, behavioral reactions, and psychophysiological reactions. Self-administered. Suitable for group use.

Scoring: Hand key; may be computer scored

Cost: 25 tests $15.00; specimen set (interpretation manual, validation studies) $5.00

Publisher: London House, Inc.

Assessment Tools for Managing Stress and Building Teamwork

OCCUPATIONAL STRESS INDICATOR (OSI)

Cary Cooper, Stephen Sloan, and Stephen Williams

Adult

Purpose: Assesses stress levels of a company's employees and identifies the causes of the stress in order to implement appropriate counseling and management programs. Used by managers in sales, warehousing, personnel, financial, data processing, marketing, and other departments.

Description: Multiple-item paper-pencil or computer-administered questionnaire measuring occupational stress. An optional Biographical Questionnaire, which can be completed in 5 minutes, is designed to elicit company and biographical information, thus providing a comprehensive picture of the group of employees being tested. A group profile is achieved using the Scoring Sheet and the Group Profiling Sheet. In addition, the Management Guide helps with interpretation of the information collected and provides examples and case studies. Other materials include an administration card, scoring keys, indicators (questionnaires), scoring sheets, and a data collection sheet. The software package allows 50 administrations. Self-administered. Suitable for group use.

Scoring: Hand key

Cost: Contact publisher

Publisher: NFER-Nelson Publishing Company, Ltd.

PIKUNAS ADULT STRESS INVENTORY (PASI)

Justin Pikunas

Adolescent, Adult—Ages 16 and older

Purpose: Measures the intensity of stress present in adults and adolescents. Used to identify individuals needing counseling in order to deal more efficiently with stress.

Description: 3-page paper-pencil inventory examining the effects of stress on the subject's personal efficiency, adjustment, and physical health. A sixth-grade reading level is required. Test results are compared to a college student sample. Self-administered. Suitable for group use.

Scoring: Hand key

Cost: Testing from $2.00; 25 forms and manual $10.00

Publisher: Justin Pikunas, Ph.D.

Assessment Tools for Managing Stress and Building Teamwork

STRESS ANALYSIS SYSTEM

P.B. Nelson, K.M. Schmidt, and Noel Nelson

Adult

Purpose: Used by adults to assess, understand, and deal with their own stress.

Description: Multiple-item paper-pencil test used by adults for developing a personal stress profile, pinpointing symptoms of stress, and managing stress. The test examines the amount of stress experienced from each of six sources: the Type A, controller personality; the anger-in personality; situational stress and life readjustments; corollary health habits; low accountability/victim syndrome; and interpersonal stress. Sell-administered. Suitable for group use.

Scoring: Self-scored

Cost: SAS Kit (test, stress profile, and stress category information) $6.50

Publisher: Interdatum

STRESS AUDIT

Lyle H. Miller and Alma Dell Smith

Adults—Ages 18 and Older

Purpose: Measures sources, symptoms, and vulnerability to stress. May be used to facilitate treatment planning in clinical setting and to identify high stress groups in corporate settings.

Description: 238-item paper-pencil or computer-administered multiple-choice test assessing the types and degree of stress an individual experiences, as well as the individual's vulnerability to stress. Six subtests containing 148 total items examine the sources of stress: Family, Individual Roles, Social Being, Environment, Financial, and Work/School. Symptoms of stress are measured by seven subscales containing 10 items each: Muscular, Parasympathetic, Sympathetic, Emotional, Cognitive, Endocrine, and Immune. Items assessing vulnerability cover life-style, health behaviors, and coping resources. Scores are yielded for each of the sources of stress subtests, symptoms of stress subtests, and vulnerability. The Stress Profile Sheet is optional. A scoring service is available from the publisher. The computer version operates on IBM PC, Apple II, and MacIntosh systems. A sixth-grade reading level is required. Examiner/self-administered. Suitable for group use.

Scoring: Computer scored; examiner evaluated; may be machine scored; self-scored

Cost: Specimen set (test booklet, profile sheet manual) $20.00

Publisher: Biobehavioral Associates

INDEX